To: Angela
To God &
For Transforming My
Story! — *BDickey*
Rom. 8:28

"My #1 *Is Still* My #1!"

by

website
www.Bernice Bright Dickey.com

xulon
PRESS

Copyright © 2010 by Bernice Bright Dickey

"My #1 Is Still My #1!"
by Bernice Bright Dickey

Printed in the United States of America

ISBN 9781615796144

All rights reserved solely by the author. The author guarantees all contents are original and do not infringe upon the legal rights of any other person or work. No part of this book may be reproduced in any form without the permission of the author. The views expressed in this book are not necessarily those of the publisher.

Unless otherwise indicated, Bible quotations are taken from The New International Version (NIV). Copyright © 1973, 1978, 1984 by Biblica; The New King James Version (NKJV). Copyright © 1982 by Thomas Nelson, Inc.; and The New Century Version (NCV). Copyright © 2005 by Thomas Nelson, Inc.

www.xulonpress.com

Dedication

This book is dedicated in memory

of
my parents,
William and Edna Delone Bright

&

of
my family,
Kevin Bernard and Naomi Eliza Dickey

Acknowledgments

First of all, I want to thank my Lord, my Strength and my Redeemer! Without Him, I would not have made it through this season of my life. ***Thank You, Jesus!***

Next, I want to thank my sisters Charlotta Bright Williams and Jeanette White Varnado who served as my gatekeepers. I love you both more than you will ever know! Miriam Anna Dickey, my beautiful daughter, and the reason for my pressing through this trial to see what the end would be. ***Mommy loves you, <u>Precious</u>***! (Smooches)

I am grateful for my Pastors, Rev. Drs. Joe and Yolande Herron-Palmore, who were a physical refuge in my time of sorrow along with the Kainos Community Church. I would also like to thank Pastors Remus and Mia K. Wright and Pastors Kirbyjon and Suzette T. Caldwell for their friendship and tremendous support.

A special thank you to all the ministries and willing vessels God used and continues to use to assist, minister, inspire, and direct me along this journey as I cross your paths. I wish that I could thank each and every one of you here but it would be impossible for me to list each name. ***All of you*** helped me and loved me back to spiritual wholeness!

Sincere gratitude is expressed to Cynthia Mulkey and Leisa Wilkins Smith for their great editorial assistance.

INTRODUCTION

In the book you are reading, you will learn what it took for me to keep my sanity and remain in my right mind while enduring tremendous emotional stress as a result of losing both my husband and oldest daughter in a collision. Many observers asked me how I was keeping it together and when I shared with them the enormous amount of time I spent in fellowship with God on a daily basis, they could not believe that *"it took all of that."*

My sanity was threatened every day because Satan was determined to take me out! I suffered through one spiritual attack after another and my only refuge was in the bosom and lap of God who gave permission for my faith to be tested. As I asked Him, ***"What now, Lord?"*** and ***"Why me?"*** I had to continually seek His face concerning the next matter in my life.

This book reflects my personal conversations with God during that first year after losing half of my family in an automobile and train accident. My prayer for you is that after reading ***"My #1 Is Still My #1!"*** you will learn the power of God's *spoken Word* over your circumstances. In this book I share my difficulties, temptations, victories, and sacrifices as **my commitment to Christ took priority over my grief.**

These transparent and revealing personal glimpses of my grief journey, combined with relevant biblical teaching, will remind you that only by putting your total trust in God can you ***"come through"*** the fiery trial of your faith!

By the first year anniversary of the accident, I was able to better indentify with Paul as referenced in **2 Corinthians 1:3-4, NIV:**

"Praise be to the God and Father of our Lord Jesus Christ, the Father of compassion and the God of all comfort, who comforts us in all our troubles, so that we can comfort those in any trouble with the comfort we ourselves have received from God."

Blessings,

Bernice Bright Dickey

CONTENTS

Acknowledgements vii

Introduction ix

JOURNAL ENTRIES

February… 15

March… 21

April… 36

May… 50

June… 65

July… 81

August… 88

September… 108

October… 118

"My #1 Is Still My #1!"

November…..131

December…..143

January…..153

"Consider it pure joy, my brothers, whenever you face trials of many kinds, because you know that the testing of your faith develops perseverance. Perseverance must finish its work so that you may be mature and complete, not lacking anything." (James 1:2-4, NIV)

FEBRUARY

2/4/02

Lord,
   I begin this journal entry as a WIDOW and A MOTHER WHO HAS LOST A CHILD!
   I begin this week as a single mother of one daughter, Miriam Anna Dickey!

On January 31, 2002, my husband, Kevin, and oldest daughter, Naomi, died in a car accident! Miriam, our baby daughter, was the only one rescued before the car exploded.

Most of my family has come to my house to be here with me and Miriam ever since they heard the tragic news of the car accident. My two sisters, Jeanette and Charlotta, along with my brother-in-law, Lawrence (Charlotta's husband), flew in from New Orleans, LA. My Uncle James, Auntie Mary Ann, Auntie Wilhemenia, and Cousin Katrina immediately drove all night from New Orleans, LA to Sugarland, TX to be here as quickly as possible for me.

Our church members met me at the hospital and have been very supportive of Miriam and myself. **All of the ministries** that Kevin and I have been affiliated with over the past 12 years have come out as well. Their prayer support and physical presence in sheer numbers has been tremendous!

2/7/02

Lord,

We are getting closer to Saturday, when I have to go through their *"CELEBRATION OF LIFE!"* It's true, it's really TRUE! Kevin and Naomi are gone and Miriam and I are left here!! I can't believe this is true! Here I am a widow who also lost a child! How can this be? You are Sovereign! You make no mistakes! Yet here I sit, alone with a baby! Miriam is healing remarkably fast and the doctor is amazed that her second and third degree burns are healing so fast! *She is my little miracle baby!*

2/9/02

Lord,

Today is their Holy Ghost Party and Celebration of Life! I feel like a party hostess, not a widow and mother who has lost a child. Since 5 A.M. I have been consecrating myself and meditating on this event, prayerfully seeking wisdom and direction from the Holy Spirit on how to proceed through this day:

1. **Suit up in my SPIRITUAL ARMOR!**
2. Look for Your footprints in the sand to walk behind You, in place of my going ahead on my own.
3. Personal prayer and devotion time alone with You to allow You to pour into me!
4. Continue to be still to allow You to minister unto me.

P. M. Revelation

Your Holy Spirit was all over the place! **I was able to stand with my full spiritual armor on today!** Your strength was magnified and glorified in the "Celebration of Life" for Kevin and Naomi Dickey! Many people were blessed beyond their own grief and were ministered to by their home going service. Again, to God be the Glory for this great thing You have done!

"My #1 Is Still My #1!"

2/11/02

Lord,

Help me! A church member has allowed the devil to ride in on him as a weak link and he is already wreaking havoc in the short time since Kevin's death only two weeks ago! He has lied repeatedly, he has stolen my original tapes of their home going service, he has kept back money received by the church on my behalf and he started rumors that I was leaving the church and going back to New Orleans, LA. He is doing all of this to get the church and to become the new Pastor. He is not our choice, yet he can't get it through his head that he is **NOT** shepherd material. He doesn't have it, not right now. You may work with him for another season but this is not his season.

On top of everything else I am dealing with – Kevin and Naomi's death, the bills being due, and caring for Miriam - now I have to do spiritual warfare even before I can properly grieve the loss of my loved ones. **Help me, Jesus!** I had Kevin and Naomi to pray with me during the last spiritual showdown in 2000. Now, it's just me and a few prayer warriors from the women's ministry left to bring down Satan's kingdom that he's trying to resurrect now that Kevin's gone. *I am not that drunk with grief* that I can't recognize this spiritual attack. I am overwhelmed by all that I am going through, but with Your help God, I will prevail in rising, standing, and praying my way through this storm.

I am awaiting the church's response on tomorrow to see how they will defend Kevin's training and preaching. Will they allow the dream to die and wither away or will they carry on the spiritual legacy Kevin left by overthrowing this oppressor who is trying to take over the church? I earnestly hope and pray that the church rises to the occasion and doesn't lie down for this fight. I modeled for them on last week how to handle this tragedy with grace and spiritual maturity. Please allow them to follow my example and to be strong enough to reject foul leadership. This is my prayer in Jesus' Name, Amen!

"My #1 Is Still My #1!"

2/20/02

Lord, God,

How excellent is Thy Name in all the earth, You are faithful to Your Name and You are absolutely mighty in battle! You showed up in a mighty way on Sunday. You exposed the devil in his schemes and it happened before the whole church. The culprit was exposed by the Holy Spirit and now can be dealt with by the leadership of the church. I am anxiously awaiting the outcome from this investigation and subsequent discipline by the governing bodies in charge. I will write You the updates as I find them out. I know that You already know how this will end.

Today I picked up Kevin's and Naomi's ashes from the funeral home. It wasn't as hard as I thought it would be. Selah. (A term used in the bible to refer to a thoughtful reflection) **I know** it was because of Your Holy Spirit comforting me and the intercessory prayers being lifted up for me and the family.

I was bristled by the death certificate from the county that stated how the accident occurred. They said that "Kevin, as the driver, attempted to go around the railroad crossing arms that were down and was hit by a train and his automobile burst into flames." To see it printed like that on his death certificate really offended me because the accident is still under investigation and I want it changed. They did not list a cause of death for Naomi. Test results are still pending and were not available as of the date of the death certificate.

I was afraid to find out that Naomi might have actually been alive while the car was burning and it disturbed me. I took it to You in prayer and You comforted me by saying that if that was so, You received her spirit and soul and what remained was only her flesh, which is dust anyway. If she was alive and only passed out and not yet dead who knows what she felt because she was passed out? I don't want to go through the mental gymnastics of figuring out if she felt her flesh burning or not. I trust that You received her and she is in a better place – **with You!** God forbid that she would have survived the accident, what would I have had to endure for the remainder of her lifetime? In Your infinite wisdom, You spared me from the morning after, thank You! When I think of the worse case scenario: Kevin was actually at fault and tried to beat the train, I come to the conclusion that You have him as well and because his death was instant he didn't feel a thing, nor did he see it coming.

You comfort me with the knowledge that You pre-ordained their births and deaths and ***You were NOT surprised by this.*** Their deaths were not untimely, but on Your schedule. **You are still in control and Sovereign.** I trust that You are working this out for my good and Romans 8:28, *"And we know that in all things God works for the good of those who love him, who have been called according to his purpose."* will show up in this tragic experience for me.

I am also waiting to fulfill my ministry calling as stated in Isaiah 61:1-3 (NIV).

¹ The Spirit of the Sovereign LORD is on me,
  because the LORD has anointed me
  to preach good news to the poor.
  He has sent me to bind up the brokenhearted,
² to proclaim the year of the LORD's favor
  and the day of vengeance of our God,
  to comfort all who mourn,
³ and provide for those who grieve in Zion—
  to bestow on them a crown of beauty
  instead of ashes,
  the oil of gladness
  instead of mourning,
  and a garment of praise
  instead of a spirit of despair.
  They will be called oaks of righteousness,
  a planting of the LORD
  for the display of his splendor.

The first two verses were given to me as the theme Scripture for the Women of Standard Ministry for our women's ministry at the church in '99 when You first called me into the ministry. Today, I am walking out verse three through the **public test** of my faith. In this test so far, I am sustained by Your peace, which surpasses all understanding, which also guards my heart and mind in Christ Jesus. (Philippians 4:7)

GOD, YOU ARE MY PEACE! Hallelujah!

Thank You for the comforting ministry of the Holy Ghost, Your Spirit! It is absolutely amazing and definitely supernatural! Continue to use me and my faith as a beacon light to others of what You can do for us, if we just trust and believe You to be there for us and have our backs! Thank You!

2/22/02

Lord God!
Continue to keep me! Keep my mind stayed on You and keep me in perfect peace! I am experiencing Your peace which surpasses all understanding and I don't want to lose it. I'm not even questioning it! I can't explain it to others either when they ask me about my peace. They must find it for themselves.

Each day that passes is another day without them and even though I have my sisters here with me, I miss Kevin and Naomi immensely! I am overwhelmed by the idea of being a single mom of a toddler. I never saw this part of the equation coming. Miriam is a normal toddler and she is into everything! I am very grateful that she is alive and here with me. I don't begrudge her, but help me Lord, not to over-indulge her because of our losses.

Lord, help me to be for Miriam what Kevin and I were together for Naomi. I know how to do the first 10 years of parenting a daughter with a partner to help me! Now, I am all alone and will have to do it again without Kevin this time and I don't know how all of this will affect Miriam. She won't have her Daddy to help raise her and he played an integral part in the molding, shaping, and training of Naomi. What will I do without Kevin's support? Lead me, guide me in every way, and send Your anointing, Father I pray, order my steps in Your Word! I'm missing Kevin a whole lot these days and then my longings shift to Nne (Naomi's nickname). Comfort me, Lord!

MARCH

3/3/02

Lord,

I told one of our members, who is also a church leader that I was called to vocational ministry three years ago and now he has to decide how to proceed with the news. I feel relieved and a burden has been lifted off of me because I have always wanted the church to know and accept me as a minister of the gospel.

My fruit has been evident throughout my tenure at the church and many have suspected for some time that I was a minister. I have only asked that they check out the fruit, my fruit remains. I thank You for sending my longtime girlfriend, Gina, from New Orleans, LA to help direct me in the path of sharing my calling now rather than waiting for a better time. Since I've done so, I don't have the stress in my neck anymore and I'm loosed! I now feel like the woman in Bishop T.D. Jakes' sermon **"Woman, Thou Art Loosed!"** You have been preparing me for this day since You anointed me and maybe I couldn't handle it before but now I am ready, is that it?

I find that in Your timing You are allowing me to grieve in intervals. Last Thursday was a difficult day for me because I visited the Bible bookstore that Kevin, Naomi, and I had visited many times before. It came upon me like a flood of emotions, but You rose up a standard against it (like a dam) to slow the flow and allow me to not be overwhelmed by the floodgates. I was driving out of the parking lot and couldn't get out before having to pull over and park to cry it out. Crying helped!

I realized what triggered it for me was visiting that bookstore for the first time without them. A place we had spent so much time and had so many memories in together as a family was now only an experience for Miriam and me. I couldn't find a book on the shelf that dealt with losing multiple family members at once and the idea about writing my own book about this bereavement experience titled, *"Miriam and me!"* came to me as I pulled out of the parking lot after crying my eyes out. (Hmm, let me think some more about that idea...)

The missing and longing feelings for my family members are intense, sometimes more intense than others, but manageable, so far, just the same. I thank You for keeping me, I thank You for comforting me, I thank You for teaching me to keep You as my Number One Love. It's because You are my Number One Love I can handle the loss of my number two (Kevin) and number three (Naomi). If it were the other way around with:

1. Kevin
2. Naomi
3. You, God

I would be an absolute nervous wreck, in a heap on the floor somewhere not able to even function. **Thank you, Jesus, for right priorities!** You taught me in my other bereavement experiences that Mom and Dad couldn't be in Your place, they had to take a back seat to You. After those experiences in '86 and '91, I learned to re-prioritize my loves and **made You - Number One!** I was married and had a child in '91 when Mom died and it wasn't as gut wrenching an experience for me because Mom was number three or four. (Nne was born in '91 so Mom was third until her birth)

I processed Mom's death a little better than I did Dad's, but it was still hard on me because I was a new mother in '91 who needed her own mother for wisdom, guidance and direction. I still miss both my parents after all of this time and I know Kevin and Naomi will be the same for me memory-wise. I am in a better place spiritually this time around when it comes to processing Kevin and Naomi's deaths. *I know* that You are Sovereign! *I know* it was Your will to allow them to die in this season of my life! *I trust* You to work this experience out for my good because I am called according to Your purpose as found in Romans 8:28. Thank You for preparing me for this time and thank You for trusting me to respond as *You* have taught me while I was in training. I still feel like I've been drafted for a special assignment in the *"Army of the Lord"* with all of the personal losses I have suffered. I have reported for duty but I am getting information on a *"need to know"* basis. So I am inquiring of You Lord, I am seeking You while You may be found, and *I expect a reward for diligently seeking You!*

3/9/02

Lord,

Even though it was an accident, apparently it was needful in order to accomplish Your purpose in our lives – individually and collectively as a corporate body for the church.

I pray for You to continue to keep me safe in Your arms. Also, keep me from emotionally feeling the full brunt of losing half of my family. Help me to keep my mind stayed on You and Your promises. Keep me still as I stand and see the salvation of the Lord. Lord, the peace that surpasses all understanding is what I am experiencing and this gift from You is what is absolutely keeping me!

Thank You for the help that comes through my family and friends who are allowing themselves to be used by You to comfort me. I am reaping what Kevin, Naomi, and I have sown over the past years and it's coming back to me – pressed down, shaken together and running over into my bosom. My question at this point in time is – why couldn't Kevin be around to see the fruit of his labor? Why was it Your will that he and Naomi had to die in order for this fruit to come forth? Our dream was for us as a family unit to experience Your prosperity – Yours was for Miriam and me to experience it alone.

I don't understand Your will and plan for my life at this juncture, nor do I understand or know why it necessitated Kevin and Naomi deaths for it to come to fruition. I trust You, God, to squeeze a Romans 8:28, *"And we know that in all things God works for the good of those who love him, who have been called according to his purpose,"* out of this for me! *"I must trust in the Lord with all my heart and lean not to my own understanding but in all my ways acknowledge Him and He will direct my path."(Psalms 3:5-6)*

My success in being strong in the Lord is in direct proportion to the amount of personal prayer and intercessory prayer support that is supplied. It is absolutely clear to me that I am engaged in spiritual warfare. This conflict is not against human forces but against a spiritual enemy. The consequences of victory or defeat are eternal, what lies in the balance is heaven or hell.

Prayer and intercession are powerful offensive weapons that greatly impact ministry. I trust that God will speak to the church family about beginning a dynamic life of prayer and that they would join in as prayer warriors with me on the battlefield for the Lord. Colossians 4:2 states *"...we should devote ourselves to prayer keeping alert in it with thanksgiving,"* that's the theme for the prayer team ministry.

God will respond to our prayers according to His will, wisdom, and amazing grace. (1 John 5:14-15) He hears the faintest cry of our hearts, the feeblest whisper of our lips, and in love He listens and responds to our faith. (Matthew 14:26-31) **Faith must focus on God** for He is the object of our faith.

3/10/02

Lord,

Thank You, Lord that I don't wake up during my sleep shaking and trembling like I did the first few weeks after the accident. You have kept me and You are keeping me and I thank You for Your keeping power! I was just reflecting on how I don't wake up in a panic anymore and realized that You answered my worst fear when I asked You the hard questions about if Kevin was at fault for the accident, and if Naomi was alive when she was burning. After we worked through those questions I was able to remain asleep and not wake up in a panic anymore – thank You!

Thank You, for counseling me and redirecting my thoughts initially after watching the accident on the news and seeing my car in flames. Hearing that Kevin and Naomi had already died and that only Miriam was rescued but in critical condition paralyzed me with great fear. I *"bargained"* with You for Miriam's life to be spared. I didn't know if You had heard me or if You had even accepted my plea. All I remember was arriving at the hospital to find Miriam alive and well with second and third degree burns on her head, neck, face, leg, and foot. She was alive! It was then that I felt You still loved me, that You heard my cry and answered my prayers. I was not going to be left alone physically in this world – Miriam was left behind. She looks just like Naomi, and she has her Daddy's head shape and features. When I look at her I see both of them and I am comforted by the fact that she's still here and in good spirits with no long term side effects from being hit by the train.

    My new concern is that Miriam is connecting with males and wanting their attention, preferring it when presented with male and female options. I have been watching her and observing that is what she does in mixed company. I wonder if it is her missing the loving affection of hugs and kisses her Daddy used to give her on a daily basis with his razor stubbed beard and hairy moustache. I pray right now that the attention seeking behavior she is doing will be diverted to You God and that she will find fulfillment in You!

    My sister Charlotta got Kevin's wedding ring cleaned up and resized to fit me and I am wearing it now. It is comforting to look down on my hand and see his ring on my finger. To wear his bracelet that is still "soot tinged" is too difficult for me right now because it reminds me of how he and Naomi died.

My sanity rests on *remembering their lives*, not their deaths!

    I choose to think on whatever is true, honorable, just, pure, pleasing, and commendable anything of excellence and worthy of praise. As I keep on doing these things, the God of peace will be with me, remain with me, and keep and sustain me. (Philippians 4:8-9)

3/10/02

11:30 P. M.

Lord,
    Can You trust me? Is that why You have allowed me to endure this trial because You trust that I could handle it and respond in a way that would give You glory? Am I on public display to demonstrate what strength in the Lord looks like? Has this been a test for the church and my trial is a by-product of their test? Remember in '91 when I kept suffering loss after loss after loss of loved ones and I wanted to know whose attention You were trying to get? Is this like that year? Are you trying to get someone's attention and it took You calling Kevin and Naomi home for it to happen? I know from reading Your Word and autobiographies that You use persons who have been *"crushed"* for Your Glory! What do You have in store for me? How will I be used for the purpose that You predestined me for? How have the visions I've seen glimpses of shaped and formed this experience I am in?

    Thank You, Lord, for keeping me, my mind, my emotions, my health, my wealth (from monetary gifts and offerings), my thoughts, and for protecting Miriam and I. Thank You for using Your angels to keep a watch over us as we slumber and rest. Thank You for being my security system, for being my refuge in this time of trouble, and for redirecting Miriam's seeking attention and affection from any male because she misses her Daddy! Thank You for directing me in the path I should go and for keeping me! Hallelujah! **You are truly AMAZING!!**

3/12/02

Lord,
    Was my experience with Dad and Mom's deaths a preparation for how to handle and respond to Kevin and Naomi's death? It seems that You trusted that I would respond in a way that would display Your glory and strength in me, as an example of the peace of God that surpasses all understanding.

I remember praying daily as "I offered my body *as a living sacrifice*, *holy and acceptable to You as my reasonable service.*" (Romans 12:1) So here I am! I also remember saying, like Mary said in Luke 1:38 when the angel appeared to her, *"Let it be with me according to your word, here am I, the servant of the Lord."*

Was this what I was submitting to when I answered Your call into ministry over two years ago on 12/7/99? Did it take my having Miriam on that same exact date one year later in 2000? Did it take growing deeper roots with You over these years through a more disciplined prayer and study time in order to serve in this assignment? Only You know! I am still waiting to hear from You. I really don't have much to say. I need to hear from You for the next step in my life! I am guessing that You have already prepared me for it, so reveal it to me now, please!

10:15 P.M.

Tonight was better than the last two nights of being alone in this house without company. Sunday, I felt the lack of physical companionship in the house and I talked on the phone all night to make up for Naomi's and Kevin's absence. Last night, I talked my ear off trying to distract myself from the fact that I was alone with Miriam. Tonight, I put Miriam down around 7 P.M. and have been enjoying my quiet time alone and have not felt the need to call up someone in order to keep me company. I have read, watched Christian television programs, and have been meditating all night and my spirit is quieted. I'm not anxious anymore about being alone in this big house tonight. I have to face this reality and the emotions that come with it one day and one moment at a time.

Miriam is recognizing her Dad's picture over the television and pointed to it on yesterday and today. That gesture really melted my heart for her to recognize him and point to him. I've realized that I will probably lose weight running after Mmi (Miriam's nickname) because I have to make up for Kevin and Naomi's absence. Thank You for working in Miriam to remember her Dad and sister. I thank You in advance for working out of her the unction to go to strange men in an attempt to compensate for her father's affection. I praise

You because *You will do this for her* and satisfy her desire for male attention and affection.

3/13/02

Lord,

Thank You, Lord, for teaching me! Thank You for teaching me how to self-feed, how to encourage myself in the Lord and how to focus on You, Your might, Your power, and Your faithfulness to Your promises to deliver that which You called into service! I'm speaking of Your calling me into full-time ministry more than two years ago and Your using women in ministry in this season. You called me and You equipped me! You also said that my gift will make room for me! I have to remind myself to be still and let You fight my battles and when I do, You work things out for my good! Thank You! Continue to keep me and my mind stayed on You and Your faithfulness. You have done so much on my behalf I don't doubt You at all!

I now see spiritually what You have to work with and through at the church. I can't believe how entrenched the strongholds, thought processes through which Satan has set up occupancy and has the advantage, are over there and realize You knew what You had to work with, *I didn't*. I thought Kevin and I were making headway and we did, it's just that weeds (devils) are sprouting up from the ground (church) and we (the prayer warriors) have to put down some spiritual "weed-n-feed" to keep back the devilish imps that are trying to uproot the good seed that Kevin and I laid down. **HELP!**

I've sent out an "S.O.S." to local area prayer teams to come out and pray with us and they have accepted. I am prayerfully anticipating and expecting Your move in the church as a result. Kevin and I made a lot of progress there, but it now seems that we hadn't made much headway with the remnant that we inherited. They are operating out of fear and are crippling the church with their dysfunction. I thought they were further along spiritually but perhaps it was only pure emotionalism.

3/14/02

Lord,

    As I receive all of the love, support and finances into my bosom, pressed down, shaken together and running over, I regret that Kevin is not alive to see this. He worked so hard, so long, so faithfully without complaining and never got to enjoy this type of outpouring of love and support of his ministry. The finances that are coming in from area churches and individuals makes me feel like I am a money magnet. We knew from reading the book *"Money Cometh"* by Leroy Thompson that money was on its way to us; we just thought it would be the BOTH (Kevin and I) of us, not just one of us! The financial support has been tremendous! I have even shared some of the money with Laverne (Kevin's mom) from the overflow. Thank You for doing exceedingly, abundantly, above all I could think to ask. As I trust in You, You are meeting my financial and physical needs as I wait for the death certificate to be corrected so that I can file the insurance claim.

    I really hate that Kevin isn't around to share in this display of appreciation. He really didn't know how many lives he impacted and neither did I. This experience has really opened my eyes. I knew we were faithful in ministry, but we never counted it up and we never knew how many lives we touched until now. Thank you for allowing Kevin and Naomi to impact others' lives. It's been awesome to see the response from all of the ministries Kevin and I worked in and with throughout the years.

    I am disappointed that the leadership at our church has chosen to respond in the same way they have in the past to the loss of their leaders. Their response is to look out for the church (by sight) rather than by faith. Consequently, they have chosen to be stingy and have reneged on their public promise of continuing to give me Kevin's salary and are operating from a place of defeat. They also want me to remain quiet and not tell the congregation that they have reneged. It's as if all of Kevin's teaching and preaching these past four years fell on deaf ears as far as they are concerned. They are operating in the flesh and not trusting God to provide for the church. As I have trusted God to meet my needs, You have raised up people to accept the challenge to bless me financially. Why can't they? Why are these church folk so stiff-necked? And why do they have a "Pharisee spirit" on them that holds the pew to a higher standard that they can't keep themselves?

The recent converts and members who joined under Kevin's leadership have been very supportive of me and Miriam and have supported me financially to make up for what the leadership of the church has taken away. They are giving me their tithes and offerings instead of the church. I told them that **the tithe belongs to YOU** and I won't accept it and that I should only receive an offering from them as a gift. This conflict about the money has caused turmoil and mess at the church due to the leadership team's decision to renege on their promise to support me and Miriam and the strongholds that are deeply rooted in them. The members want to support me directly if the church won't give me the money as they promised. I pray that all intercessory prayers would blow the strongholds apart, disintegrate them, and crush them down never to arise again. God has already said we win in spiritual warfare, so let's do this!

3/20/02

Lord,

I fear being a single mom to Miriam. I never wanted to raise my children alone but with my husband, their father! Kevin is gone and I wonder if I can do as good a job as we did together with Nne. I feel overwhelmed by this assignment and I know I need You at this time and every step of the way. I pray every day that You will leave footprints in the day to show me the path that I should go for that day. I need to feel Your presence, Lord. All I feel is alone without Kevin and Naomi. Miriam and I don't feel complete without our other half of the family. I know You didn't make a mistake. I know that **YOU KNOW** what You are doing. I know, I know, I know! But right now, I don't know what to do? Now what? Where do I go from here?

On January 31st, I woke up a wife and mother of two daughters, today I am a widow with one daughter. On January 31st, I was a co-laborer in ministry with my husband, a partner joined at the hip, today I'm being prepared to do ministry by myself without him. On January 31st, I trusted You; *today I **still** do trust You!*

Thank You for keeping me! Thank You for keeping my inner man, my spirit, alive while my flesh dies daily. Thank You for keeping me focused on You and not my current circumstances. You are definitely the One who is in control and in charge of my days. You order my steps and keep me sane. You keep my mind regulated, and You are fixing my heart, mending it while I'm out on Family Medical Leave and thereafter. This time of reflection and redirection I'm experiencing is for this season. I need the time off to assess my situation, listen to You, and plan for the next step and level You have for me.

I miss my husband and Nne! I miss what we used to be. I miss what we had, and who I was with them. I miss being Kevin's wife and Nne's Mom. I guess I will always be that, but they aren't here now, just Miriam and I remain of our earthly family. My husband, my good husband, my devoted husband, my doting husband, my only husband is gone! He made me feel like a queen! I was honored! I was loved by that man! He made me enjoy being married to him! My Nne was a model child. She was obedient, smart, artistic, and athletic and she was mine! She was my first baby, my look-alike, my little helper, my angel of mercy, my prayer warrior, my cheerleader, my imitator, my pride, mommy's baby girl even though she was growing up. She made being her Mom look easy and feel easy. I miss my family! I really, really, really, miss them! It's been seven weeks since their accident and their absence is deafening to me. Even with all the calls and visitors, I still miss their presence. Selah.

I look at our pictures and remember what we had and know that I'll never be the same. The married *"Bernice"* with two children died on that day. The **new** *"Bernice"* with one child and a widow is still emerging from the ashes. I see glimpses of her in my spirit but the picture isn't all together clear to me today. Sometimes I see her clearer than on other days, today I long for the married Bernice more than I want to be the widowed Bernice. My heart is heavy as I move through the day and see people who still have their spouses and wonder why our time was so short. We had planned for more time together, more ministries together, and more life together. I look back on my pictures of us as a family and miss it. Me and Miriam are together now and have to take some more pictures to establish our new family and create new memories.

3/22/02

Lord,

    Thank You for ordering my steps to Kainos Community Church on tonight. You ministered mightily to me and poured into my <u>*absolutely empty*</u> vessel! I did not realize how spiritually parched I was until I received a downpour of Your love and kindness from the Daughters of Kainos Women's Ministry. I was ministered to in a way that I have not even received at my own church ever since the accident. *It was way past due for <u>me</u> to be ministered to and absolutely necessary!*

    You used my friends, Mia Wright and Yolande Herron-Palmore, to minister to me along with the other women from the fellowship. They sat me down in a chair and all of the women came around me and laid their hands where they could all over me. Then, they prayed for emotional healing from my losses and interceded for wisdom and direction for my future ministry. They travailed so strong in prayer for me; it was as if they were all in labor to birth *<u>me</u>!* I felt the spirit of heaviness being supernaturally pulled up off of me like clothes over my head! The only way that I can explain it is like this, they were used like spiritual sponges that sopped up all the emotional pain, sorrow, and heartache that I had been feeling up until that point. The women interjected themselves between me and the fiery darts that I had been receiving and formed an impenetrable wall between me and Satan. For the first time since the accident, I felt covered in spiritual warfare for my faith in God and I didn't want them to leave me! Their prayer ministry physically relieved me of the stress I was feeling and raised me up out of the depression over the overwhelming loss of everything from Kevin and Nne's deaths, to the mess at my church and the leaders rejecting my call into vocational ministry.

    As I reflected on everything on the way home from this fellowship, I realized that You have provided relief for me in other ways, too! I recognized that I am not struggling financially (light bulb moment)! *Even as I am going through this very excruciating emotional ordeal, You have already provided for me and Mmi financially!*

I remembered how Kevin and I sowed multiple financial seeds of tithes and offerings for many years. I finally recognize that I am experiencing that seed sowing harvest coming back to me now through Your ambassadors. My realization of Your faithfulness to Your Word when we give to You as instructed, has been uplifting to me as well, Lord! In spite of everything else I am going through, You have remained true and faithful to Your Word! (Luke 6:38) Hallelujah!

3/26/02

Lord,

Thank You for sending me home to New Orleans to be ministered to by my own family. You ordered my steps to New Orleans, I thought to intercede on my grandfather's behalf, but it was to get me to a place (home) where I would continue to be restored and poured into like I was at Kainos Community Church the other night.

I didn't realize how drained I was of energy by the things I was going through at my own church until I got here and began to be filled by Your nourishing Spirit. Not being comforted by my own church made me extremely famished for emotional and spiritual support. I was weary in well-doing and was growing faint. Isaiah 41:10 states *"...that God will strengthen me..."* and I feel it now that I am away from my own church.

I am anointed to walk in victory for the trials I am destined to go through in this year. I understand that the battle is not mine, but the Lord's. (2 Chronicles 20:17) I am in tremendous spiritual warfare but I know we are the winners! The process of standing on Your Word grows tiresome in this flesh but to God be the Glory for strengthening me! The devil is seeking to take over my home church and after the loss of Kevin, the late shepherd of that church, he seeks to devour the sheep. Lord, I still have a shepherd's spirit and I am willing to continue on with your sheep until my watch is over. Your will, not mine be done in this matter, Lord!

I was left behind with a mission yet to accomplish, even if Satan had permission to sift me and was allowed to take Kevin and Naomi out of this world. Kevin's season is over. He is in a better place, a place of reward for his labor at the church and the many years before that. God, You are Sovereign and You are in control! You are yet on the throne! Keep my mind stayed on You, give me the game plan for my life and the courage to carry it out! Please strengthen the camp (church) so that they will follow You and not cave in to the fear and intimidation of the devil who is roaring like a lion at the church. Have them to tremble yet STAND in the Name of Jesus!! Amen!

3/28/02

Lord,

Could a focus of K & N Dickey Ministries, Inc. be a scholarship fund for the Christian schools like Nne attended? Christian schooling along with the consistent teachings at home contributed to her depth and understanding of the Word of God that was evident in her journal writings at age eight shared in the funeral program. I'm also considering funding a stipend for bi-vocational ministers. Ministers, like Kevin, who weren't able to obtain outside support financially because their church had tapped out all available local financial resources and were still struggling with nothing to show for it, like our church.

Kevin and I struggled financially because of that blight on the church and not being able to access resources from organizations like Union Baptist Association (UBA). But You delivered us anyhow, Hallelujah! You said in Your Word in Psalms 34:19 that, *"Many are the afflictions of the righteous, but the Lord delivers us from them all,"* thank You! We were sincere in our efforts to train up disciples at the church and many seeds have been planted there.

As I think of all the details that contributed to a spiritually strong Dickey family, I could write a book on it and then teach the principles in a seminar setting! Is that my focus as President of K & N Dickey Ministries, Inc.? I'm still seeking a focus for the ministry that You gave me to memorialize Kevin and Naomi and to continue the Dickey Family Legacy. You showed me that I could preserve the ministry that Kevin and I began together apart from any church affiliation through the birthing of **K & N Dickey Ministries, Inc.,** a 501(c)(3), non-profit organization! Thanks! Now I can let go of my fight to maintain Kevin's legacy at the church because I will continue it outside of any church affiliation.

I was driving Charlotta's car late last night looking for a place to buy another pacifier for Miriam and drove past the La Quinta Inn that the Dickey Family stayed at in December '01 last year when we came to New Orleans for Charlotta's graduation. I came across pictures from the graduation and we all were so alive, intact, and together! Who knew that that visit would be our last as a family? My next visit to New Orleans was in January '02 when I came to be with Charlotta and Jeanette during Jeanette's kidney donor transplant operation for a member of her church. Now my follow-up visit to that one is with Miriam on this trip without Kevin and Naomi as we visited our favorite relative – *Grandpa!* He is doing well considering he has a blood clot in his lung. He is 82 and still holding on!

APRIL

4/2/02

Lord, Lord, Lord...

I feel like the bubble You had me insulated in is losing air, it's seeping out and I am becoming deflated. I am beginning to feel my pain and I thought that the peace I enjoyed that surpassed all understanding was *Your gift to me for this entire trial.* I thought that it wasn't just for a season of grief, but for the whole process of grief. Now that family and friends have stopped rearranging their schedules, the cards and calls have stopped coming in, and the visits have stopped, it's just me and Mmi and You!

I feel my emotions and the tears well up in me. I feel the lump in my throat and I swallow the pain back down. I feel the sinking feeling in the pit of my stomach and the trembling in my body again that wakes me up out of my sleep. I thought You conquered that symptom in me, why is it returning? The peace that sustained me and the strength I felt **were true** at the time after the accident, but now I feel like I am falling apart!

I can't be REAL at my own church because they haven't been ministering to me, but I to them! It's me, Lord that needs to be ministered unto and comforted! I need wisdom to manage this conflict! I need restoration! I need to be poured into! I need to be healed!

Before visiting Kainos Community Church on 3/22/02, I felt drained, but I'm being revived the longer I stay away from my own church. What does that mean Lord? Is this the time to leave or is this

"My #1 Is Still My #1!"

just a respite, like a furlough, from battle before I have to suit up and go back in for the next battle? Help me to discern Your will in this matter and give me the courage to be obedient.

I have a question **for You,** why does my (observed to be strong) spiritual maturity level in Christ cause them (at my church) to **not know how to minister to me?** What does my spiritual level have to do with ministering to me? I am still human and I need prayer as well as support! Lord, minister to me through willing vessels who understand my frailty despite my (perceived) maturity level. ***Please! Help Me!***

I need to comprehend that Kevin and Naomi's part in my story is over!! Their part in my destiny is over!! **My destiny is NOT tied to them because they are gone!** If it were, they would not be gone but here to share my future. **They are DEAD!** I need to wash my face, accept the will of God and move on – but I need Your help to let them go, to move on to my destiny. I know the motto in our marriage was *"The Best is Yet to Come,"* but how? Now I have to see this best that's yet to come out of this without my husband and daughter. We had planned to spend our lives together, our vision for ministry was together – what we thought would be our destiny as a family intimately.

My stomach is still churning as I try to process my destiny not including Kevin and Naomi in my future. I know You have ordered my steps, that You are in control, and this tragic accident didn't just happen!! It was Your will even in this separation due to their deaths. My pain is still in Your will. It didn't just happen!! You are orchestrating this for my good. (Romans 8:28)

What do the numbers (10) and (38) mean in numerology for You? Kevin was 38, Nne was 10, and we were married for 12 years. Do these numbers have meaning and significance?

I thank You for the provision that You have made through my tax refund! I can make it for the next two months and pay taxes that are due after paying my tithes. (I pay tithes off of my offerings received) I'm still giving tithes to the church (even though we are in strife) since I'm still there and You haven't released me yet. I have seeded offerings into some of the ministries that Kevin and I always wanted to support but didn't have the extra funds to do so before. It's great to be able to finally contribute to them. I have begun the sharing of the overflow and I await Your direction for this month's offering.

4/5/02

Lord,

Thank You for leading me to the Prayer Explosion at Windsor Village United Methodist Church yesterday and today. The prayer support I received was tremendous and exactly what I needed as I returned from New Orleans and am in the process of preparing for Nne's birthday party this weekend.

The insights that I received in New Orleans were liberating: I need to let Kevin and Naomi go, and I need to move on and find a new church home. The phrase that has helped me as I process my loss of Kevin and Naomi is, *"my loss is their gain,"* and that really sobered me up to realize the truth of that phrase. I am being selfish to ask them to return and I know they're in a better place and would not want to return to this side. *__I know this!__* It's the same realization I had to come to with Momma and it helped me to release her. I pray as I go through this grieving process that You will keep me, hold me, and bring me back when I let go and let my spirit grieve my losses.

I talked to one of the leaders at the church tonight and vented my frustrations to him about what I have experienced at the church and he agreed that everything I stated was true, but the only consolation he offered was to forgive them and move on. I have forgiven the leaders for their immaturity and insulting behavior demonstrated to me during this process. But I still hold them accountable for their actions and challenge them to grow up fast because it's needful and past time to do so! I have too much work to do on myself with the grieving process to spend energy on God's business *and His church* (before Kevin and I ever heard about them). Only God can keep Kevin's legacy alive and stop the cankerworm from eating up all Kevin and I have planted in the people at the church! *Do it!*

I feel doubly relieved by these decisions I have made and I plan on visiting other local churches to get my spiritual nourishment and emotional healing as I travel through this season. It's been two months and I am beginning to feel my loss. I am drawn back to

"My #1 *Is Still My #1!*"

1/31/02 when I saw my car on fire and realized that they said Kevin and Naomi had already died and Miriam alone was saved! I can't believe that they really are gone and that they won't be returning home! It's final and I can, **no must**, divide up their ashes and let their dust go. Can I? Am I ready? Is it time?

4/8/02

Well Lord, I did it!!

I shared their ashes with our family this weekend. I opened up the urns and filled the family's vials and gave them up. A huge step for me? You bet!! I'm beginning to let go. I didn't find Kevin's gold tooth in the ashes yet. They won't be walking through the door – at all! I brought them home as ashes! I'm getting it! That's proof that they are gone!

Charlotta and Jeanette visited this weekend and their presence really helped me. It was very hard for me to go through Nne's birthday weekend without her. In memory of her, we worked the Special Olympics in my school district. Then I had a birthday party for her later that day on Saturday with family and friends. I did OK on April 6th. April 7th was more difficult for me because that date was her actual birthday. I allowed myself the room to grieve, I cried most of the day.

On April 6th, I went up to the church with some of the ladies from the Women of Standard Ministry to get Kevin's things from his office and to pick up their funeral displays. I was harassed by one of the hostile church leaders who showed up to watch me while I was packing up my husband's things and all I could do was pray for self-control not to go off on him! I asked You silently, what should I do? Should I call the police on him for harassing me? I was counseled by the ladies from our Women of Standard Ministry to just let it go and ignore him. What was his problem? He truly needs Jesus!!

I made it back to church on Sunday, April 7th, only to be surprised by the ladies of the Women of Standard Ministry who had renovated the children's room and rededicated it as the ***Naomi Dickey Christian Education Center*** for the church. I was overwhelmed to say the least and speechless (to boot). I know the level of spiritual warfare they had to go through in order to accomplish this feat and that really moved me to tears, gut wrenching tears that wouldn't stop.

My grief drove me to praise and worship YOU! It really did relieve me of the stress I was feeling trying to hold it all together. It allowed me to release Nne a little more when I realized that the room was in her honor and memory. It's beautifully done in lavender and white with furnishings and children's books and games. One wall has her picture along with her journal writings from the program we gave out at the funeral. The room makeover looks wonderful, and it means more to me than the Women of Standard will ever know. I know what they were up against (hostile church leaders) and to see them come together to pull this off for the Dickey/Roberts family really made an impression on me. It really made me proud (like a Momma) to see the level of spiritual maturity and courage they had to display in order to complete this endeavor. **My ladies rallied together on my behalf and persevered! Hallelujah!** So what do I do now, Lord? Where do I go from here? I plan to leave this church and now I have this soul tie to the church? What now?

Lord, I pray for You *to help me* to endure the continual offenses that I encounter from the leadership team at the church while You perfect that which concerns me. I need You to keep me walking in the Spirit as they walk in the flesh against the Spirit of God in me. Help me to walk in wisdom and love as I endure this season of testing until my positive change comes, Hallelujah! You are my Awesome God, there is none like You! I found myself **worshiping You** on my most difficult day, April 7th, 2002, Naomi's 11th birthday. How about that?!

You, Lord, inspire me!
You, Lord, encourage me!
You, Lord, minister to me!
You, Lord, keep me!
You Lord, hold me!
You, Lord, You, Lord, only You!
There is none like You!

4/10/02

Lord,
From the vision You have given me for **K & N Dickey Ministries, Inc.** You have developed three goals for the ministry:

1) Preaching
2) Reaching
3) Teaching

Preaching – Kevin's sermon tape sales will finance the stipend for Pastors of small churches to help them out financially until their church can take care of them financially.

Reaching – Book sales of Nne's prayer journal entries will finance scholarships for families who are middle class wage earners like we were who desired their kids to have a **Christian** elementary school education.

Teaching – I will teach on how to nurture Christian families in these challenging times.

4/15/02

Lord,
Help me to release the church into Your hands. I want to clearly discern Your voice as You direct me where You would have me to worship. *I can not remain, nor finance, nor support wicked, evil leadership. I have to get out of there and soon!*

4/16/02

Lord,
Hollow! That's how I'm feeling, absolutely hollow, like a shell with all the life force sucked out. I lack energy and want to sleep the days and nights away. I want help, I want to be ministered to, but I don't have the energy to reach out and ask for it. Lord, I accept all offers of help right now, and solicit prayer support from everywhere

to carry me through this season *(my whisper prayer from my heart to Yours)*.

On last Wednesday, 4/10/02, I went to Naomi's school, Light Christian Academy, to accept her basketball team jersey. They had retired her number (11) and all the students were wearing her number (11) on their team jerseys in memory of her this season. It was a very moving, beautiful ceremony *(I need to get a copy of the videotape)*. Today, 4/16/02, I went to Naomi's pediatrician's office where they dedicated the *"Reach Out and Read"* Literacy Program in their office in memory of her. The Governor's wife and the media all came out for this dedication. We have pictures with every body as keepsakes.

I am hollow, empty, scooped out, and physically alone! I realized that the opportunities I have had to memorialize Naomi were because <u>SHE-IS-DEAD</u>!

I know if Nne were alive these moments would not have been, so I'm hurting! I miss my baby girl. She was only ten years old chronologically, but spiritually and maturity-wise she was older. In my flesh I'm devastated! In my spirit I am rejoicing that I taught her well enough to choose You before she died! And she did! I know she's with her Daddy. They not only died together, but went to heaven together as well, Hallelujah! Miriam and I are left to take another chariot to heaven later on in this lifetime.

I finally received the amendment to their death certificates. It now states that they were in an auto-train collision and died. I found out from the death certificate that Nne died from her internal injuries, not from the burns – **Praise the Lord**! They both were charred, the car was charred, yet Miriam escaped along with some personal effects salvaged from the car.

When I think of the contradiction of these two things my mind shuts down. I can't go any further in my thinking. Here I sit with Miriam and the ashes from Kevin and Naomi, my reality is two urns of ashes and one **very alive** infant!! **Help!!** I holler out in my flesh when I get to this point of dichotomy because I don't get it! I don't know how to move forward!

The calendar is marching forward, but in my reality I am maybe on February 1st, 2002 running back to January 31st, 2002 when I had a family with a husband and two daughters.

4/17/02

Lord,
Thank You for meeting me today! In my Bible study on the integrity of Joseph you taught me how ***NOT TO ALLOW*** bitterness to consume me. All of the Bible study I did today was on how to overcome bitterness and how not to allow it to get inside of me in preparing for my next level. In all of my disciplines today: my meditation, my witnessing to a fellow saint, my personal worship time, my praise of You being Jehovah – Rapha *and* my Hallelujah, You absolutely ministered to me throughout the whole day and released me through my praise of all of the stress I was feeling in my neck, shoulders, and back. Thank You, thank You, thank You!!

I realized through watching my Christian videos that You absolutely had to allow me to go through this so that I may become an empty shell that only You could use for Your Glory! My hollow feeling on yesterday was Your orchestration so that I would come to this point of yieldedness and submission to be effectively used in Your service. It's my decreasing and deflating and Your increasing and inflating me with Your Holy Spirit that makes me useful in Your Kingdom. Thank You for giving me this revelation through Your ministry servants, Veron Ashe and Jackie McCullough, on tonight through the videos from The Koinonia Fellowship 2001. They were inspirational and revived my Spirit – Hallelujah! I learned to start my day with Hallelujah to put the enemy on notice that my Jehovah reigns!! Amen!!

4/18/02

Lord,
A neighbor who attends Abundant Life Cathedral invited me to their women's fellowship cell group tonight. No one knew me there except for the lady who invited me and I didn't share my loss with

the group. I was not led to tell them about the accident only that I had recently lost two loved ones and I knew how to handle my loss because I have been through this before.

I was poured into so deeply by my fellowship with You and the videos from last night that it strengthened me enough to get through tonight's fellowship. I listened as the other ladies shared their pain and I didn't feel compelled to *"best"* them with my own trial. God already had met me and the Holy Spirit had ministered to me earlier today. Thank You for leading me in what to share and when to share. In time God, You will lead me to whom and to what ministries You want me to tell my story to.

4/20/02

Lord,

You have been showing me that this trial is not about finances for me, but Your provision *for* me. I looked back on the past two months bank statements and saw that I had received more in love offerings than Kevin and I earned together monthly! I have been home, and *Kevin went home* to be with You – and You provided for this widow and her daughter! You have met my needs for the month of May exceedingly, abundantly, above all I could ask or *think* to ask! To You, God, be the Glory for being Jehovah-Jireh, my Provider! Hallelujah!

My trust in You, Lord, is what will bring me through! As I meditate and pray in my Spirit, You give me clarity on the "processing" I'm going through – thank You!

4/22/02

Marvelous Monday!!

What a time we had on tonight with You, Lord! It was absolutely wonderful to be at the Fountain of Praise! The message was *"My Gift is About to Be Opened."* It walked all up and down my experience since the accident. It was as if You told the speaker my business. But what happened was the Holy Spirit worked the room and got all up in my face with what is about to happen in and through me. It will be an AWESOME WONDER how a ministry came out of this tragic experience! "**...BUT GOD!**"(*Another possible title for a book on this experience*) knows what He is doing and orchestrated all the details from the beginning and He's still in control. Thank You, Lord for healing my broken heart through praise and worship.

Every time I worship You, *every time I worship You, You heal me!* You are Jehovah-Rapha, the Sovereign One, who makes all my bitter experiences sweet! You are El-Shaddai, the Almighty Breasty One in whose bosom I am comforted! Hallelujah!

My last fellowship with the Women of Standard Ministry helped me to move through my grief over the mistreatment I experienced from the church leadership team. The truths I learned were:

1. God is allowing their rude behaviors to manifest to show me what was really in the hearts of the people who were acting out.
2. What's in you will come out of you when life puts the squeeze on you.
3. If I'm passionately concerned for God's people, just think **how much *more* He is passionately concerned** and He cares about what's going on and will redeem His people.

This is my prayer God:

*If this church **ever** was Your church, redeem it! If not, tell all the saints of God to get out of the way before Your wrath comes forth!*

4/26/02

What do I hope to receive at this Daughters of Kainos women's retreat? *(Question posed to those of us attending).*

I hope to receive continued peace about my decision to move on and leave my home church. I hope to receive confirmation that the decision came from You (God) with an unction from the Holy Ghost. I want confirmation of what You've been saying to me since a week ago Friday. I realized that a new Pastor at the church would lead

"My #1 Is Still My #1!"

them in a different direction than where Kevin and I were leading them and had to ask myself, "Could I sit under this new vision?"

It was then I realized that Kevin's and my vision for ministry could continue separated from the church in the 501(c)(3) Ministry started by myself as a memorial to my family. It was at that time I felt a release spiritually from my home church and that I could walk away and the church could go on without the Dickeys. It was time for the new team to come in and our season was over. My destiny doesn't include Kevin *or* that church.

My spiritual condition is one of brokenness in spirit and a contrite heart. I feel the need to stand under Your "fountain of praise" to be restored and healed of my broken heart. I am here to soak up the Word of God like a sponge and to worship You. I want to receive another breakthrough as I fellowship with You. I thank You for moving me from being stuck in a grieving mode. As I phoned one of the church leaders today and apologized for my acting out towards the leadership team while I was grieving, I felt a spiritual weight lifting up and dropping off of me. I felt the demonic spirits that had settled in me through the root of bitterness exit me because I humbled myself and apologized for the part I played in the misunderstanding at the church in this season of shared mourning.

I'm free and feel loosed from the emotional bondage I had due to my expectations not being met and my disappointment with the leadership team at the church. I've accepted that they were spiritually immature and were not capable of giving me what I needed at a critical time in my life and that is why they let me down. **But God DIDN'T!** Thank You for refocusing me on You and not on what I didn't get! I rehearsed in my mind **what I did receive from You** through other people and ministries and You more than made up for their lack, Hallelujah! I thank You for getting my nose in joint, heaven in my view, and faith as my guide that this too shall pass.

From the retreat so far, I realized that this church mess doesn't weigh in on my eternal destination. I need to remember that I'm a citizen of heaven traveling through and I don't need to entangle myself with earthly affairs. This battle isn't mine, but the Lord's and I'm out of it, and out of the way. Thank You for helping me to see that I was overly involved with matters at the church and that

You've got it! My assignment is to raise Miriam and do the ministry You have called me to do and anything else **You** call me to do in the future. I'm at peace now because I've taken my seat! Hallelujah!

4/29/02

Jesus, I am in pain! I'm physically hurting and I can't stay asleep without my flesh feeling weak and grasping the magnitude of my loss. I mourned deeply in my sleep – so deeply that I woke myself up and began crying, *"Lord, help me!"*

I recognize that the energy I spent being mad at the church leadership was a diversion from doing the emotional work I need to do on myself and when I walk away from the church there will be no excuse for *NOT* dealing with me and my response to this tragedy. Miriam will be in school, I will be back at work but the truth of the matter is this - *I will still be a recently widowed, single mom of a baby, who has also lost her first baby!*

Lord, I need help to process my grief! I have made some strides on my own, but I will need "spiritual" midwives to help me on this journey. Lord, hear my prayer, Oh Lord, hear my prayer!! I ache...I need...Lord, Lord, Lord, *please help me!!*

From the retreat this weekend, I learned that this trial has made me pregnant with possibilities and this retreat experience is my preparation spiritually for my anointing, **Your call on my life**! I am on the verge of another breakthrough, and I am highly favored of the Lord. (Luke 1:30) I am pregnant with myself, I am about to give birth to myself. My spiritual appetite has changed! I only want to be with You! I only want to hear from You! I can't get enough of You!! You have turned my appetite to You and You Alone! Hosanna! The more I seek You, the more I learn of You – **You are SO HUGE!** As I pour out my spirit to You – You fill me with Your Spirit – Thank You! When I come back from fellowshipping with You, I realize that I can't go back the way I came and I can't stay where I am. I don't know what the future holds but **I TRUST YOU** to keep me and bring me through – Hallelujah! Minister Renita Weems said at the retreat that I am pregnant with possibilities when all hell breaks loose – which it has in regards to my church home.

Reflecting back on the Prayer Vigil we held on February 1st, at the church, I realize that Kevin's mantle was passed on to me in the service and I was "commissioned as a *general*" in the army of the Lord. I am still receiving my orders and preparing to execute this assignment with precision. God called me by name – *"Bernice Marie"* – He created me, formed me (fashioned me, shaped me), according to Isaiah 43:1. When God speaks to me, something inside of me shifts back to its original place that was deposited before the foundation of time. He reaches down to the core and essence of me and restores me. I heal, I become solidified, I become whole again because I am lining up with my destiny, my purpose for coming to earth.

In this experience, I continue to long to return to heaven to be with my family. I have more family members on that side (heaven) than over here. I want to complete whatever assignment You have called me to and <u>*DO IT*</u>! So that I can return home to be with Jesus as soon as I finish it! This experience has really set my affections on heaven and my desires to move through this life also known as "vapor" as quickly as possible. I miss Kevin and Naomi, but I enjoy Miriam's company also. Help me to sort through this experience, Lord!

Also at the retreat I received confirmation that dysfunctional relationships will make you feel that you have to *"feel"* a release before you can leave the relationship. I learned that God speaks through "synchronicity" – confirmation of a decision you have made through bill boards, radio, retreats, wise counsel, etc. and for me that settled in my spirit like an anchor.

Yesterday at my home church, the leadership team went out of their way to be kind to me, which confused me momentarily because I thought it was a sign that they could really care for me. I immediately rebuked the devil for he alone knew of my decision and was trying to trick me. Thank You for clarity and sober mindedness after a mountain top experience over the weekend. Thank You!! As the theme for our weekend retreat stated: *I AM A WOMAN OF FAITH: WATCH OUT MOUNTAIN! (Matthew 17:20)*

As I reflect on my experiences I can't help but see how I have come full circle. When I first came to Houston, I joined Brentwood

Baptist Church where I met Rev. Yolande Herron-Palmore and her husband, Joe Palmore (he wasn't a minister at that time). I also met Rev. Herbert Brisbane, the Singles Minister, (who later married Kevin and me out of that ministry) and his wife Wanda.

Now, 17 years later, I am going back to my spiritual mentors for guidance and direction in this grieving experience. Rev. Yolande and her husband now Pastor a church here in Houston (Kainos Community Church) and Rev. Brisbane ministers across the U.S. as a UBA Mission's Pastor/leader. They both knew me when I was a babe in Christ and now they are serving as my spiritual "midwives" to birth me through to my next level in ministry, calling, and anointing. They are still my coaches, my angels like Gabriel was to Mary in Luke, your messengers telling me that I am truly pregnant with possibilities in the midst of this trial.

Lord, Jesus, help me please, as I continue to go through this grief process!!

MAY

5/7/02

Lord,

I've been back at work two days today and You were definitely carrying me! I listened to Creflo Dollar tonight and he said that I am anointed to go through this season because You called me to this assignment. I did it! I made it through the *first* day back, no matter how difficult, and I pressed through and now I'm two days down with Your help and the tremendous prayer support I receive from Your vessels willing to be used by You to intercede on my behalf. Thank You for loving me through others. I feel You present and near me through their service to me. I've been looking back on these past three months and I see how much You have provided for me through others – financially, physically, materially, emotionally, spiritually, psychologically, presently, and continually. There is no way to explain it other than El Shaddai was in the House! Almighty God is carrying me and to God be the Glory for taking care of His own.

    I was given information for WIC and Food stamps to help me out financially, **but I don't want our testimony to be marred. I want to testify that** *You moved on the hearts of Your people and <u>You cared for me completely</u> through them!* **Amen and Hallelujah!**

"My #1 Is Still My #1!"

5/12/02

Lord,

I went to church on Friday night because I was spiritually *flat*, desiring to be filled with Your Holy Spirit and desperately seeking intimacy with You. I went up to the altar for prayer and <u>DID NOT</u> receive anything more than I already had.

But God!

You met me in the parking lot during intercessory prayer among close friends and *Your anointing* fell on me and *filled me with Your Spirit **AGAIN**!* I was restored! I felt full and not empty and was strong in my spirit man ***AGAIN!*** Thank You for filling me up again! Thank You for meeting me at church! And thank You for being faithful to reward me for diligently seeking You!

You looked out for me today as well when I went to Pastor Cofield's (He did the eulogy for my family) church for Mother's Day and I was "topped off" in my spirit. Thank You for giving me just what I needed to make it through this Mother's Day weekend! You strengthened me and kept me in spite of this being my ***first*** Mother's Day with out Kevin and Naomi. YOU WERE AWESOME ON THIS DAY, ALMIGHTY GOD!! Thank You! To God Be the Glory for helping me through this Mother's Day! And thank You for refocusing me on Miriam and what I have to be grateful for - **Miriam is still ALIVE and *I am still a mother!* Hallelujah!**

5/15/02

Lord, Lord, Lord,

It's on You! I want to interfere and help You out but You have exercised self-control in me – **to keep my mouth *shut*** - until You allow me to speak up and out. The situation at my home church has become very interesting; the fellow who was serving in the interim position pulled out as interim and jumped into the ring for the Pastorate. The leadership team seems to think he is OK! But I discern that he had this agenda from the beginning in relation to the

Pastorate. He doesn't support women in leadership and has told me that I need to make a decision about leaving the church when *he becomes the Pastor!*

I thank You for keeping me, for strengthening me, and for healing me emotionally!! I'm feeling stronger everyday since I was slain in the Spirit Friday night in New Light Christian Center's parking lot. When I came to, You had anchored me and my faith, again. You had steadied me and planted my feet <u>AGAIN</u>! **Hallelujah!**

Work this week has been better; I can feel the prayer support and know that You are allowing these things to happen (in season) to me. The purpose of these additional trials is still being revealed. I am sure that You are still in control and You've got this. Thank You for Peace and Rest!

5/19/02

4 P. M. Revelation

Lord,

I went to a Women's Retreat at Del Lago Resort sponsored by Southwest Community's Women's Ministry this weekend and I felt a spiritual closure on my issues with my home church. I can't go down to the altar for prayer anymore on this matter. ***It is done!*** I also felt an emotional closure on my grief over this. I went down to the altar for prayer and deliverance and felt that I was at the altar without cause because my emotional healing was released to me earlier that day in the prayer prayed for release from pain! Hallelujah! Thank You for working through others to minister to me and to coach me through this season. I feel Your Love through the arms of my sisters in Christ in all the women's ministries who have nurtured me throughout this grief journey!

While in church at Kainos today, I heard You say that I've been hiding behind Kevin and working in ministry with him when I was suppose *"to do"* the ministry You called me to do. You allowed me to work alongside of him for a season but that season was over and ***NOW* it's time for us (You & Me) to MINISTER!** I heard all of this before church even started. It's time for my coming out party/debut. It's about You and Me, now there's room for <u>YOUR</u> ministry because I'm not working in Kevin's ministry. I'm moving from where we ministered together and starting all over in a NEW PLACE! I pray for wisdom and direction of where You would have me to move to for ministry!

Tonight I have a meeting with the church leaders to reconcile our differences and plan for my departure. I pray for FAVOR!!

11:36 P. M. Revelation

Thank You for a productive meeting with the church leadership team! I was able to dialogue with them about my hurts and they admitted their shortcomings in regards to meeting my needs (not attending to me). They agreed to recognize Kevin's contributions to the church (soon) in a public way and to allow me to make the announcement to the church regarding my departure and future absences on Sundays! Reconciliation happened and I can go in peace – regarding my decision to leave! Thank You for answering my prayers, **Hallelujah!**

I also polled them on how they felt about women preachers and every last one of them felt that **I WOULD NOT** be allowed to preach at the church because of their collective stronghold regarding women preachers. They won't argue with my call to the ministry but stated I needed to exercise that gift elsewhere (not at *their* church) and they would support my moving on! (*I was not surprised.*) So in essence, I made them feel like they helped me to make a decision on where to go and what to do with my ministry gifts.

Thank You for helping me to walk away with grace and dignity. Thank You for arranging this meeting for such a time as this and for giving me favor in my request of them to honor Kevin's legacy at the church. I pray that the recognition they plan will not take too long to happen and would include everyone in the church so as not to leave anyone out of the loop and unawares.

Order my steps to my next church home, Lord! Lead me and guide me in everyway, let me feel Your anointing, Father I pray, order my steps in Your Word!

5/22/02

Lord,

Today I learned by reading the witnesses' account of the accident that Naomi *was still alive after the collision and that she burned to death!* She was pinned in and couldn't be rescued from the vehicle. She was moaning and going in and out of consciousness when the fire consumed her. **Kevin *was* dead on impact, but Nne wasn't. According to the witnesses, she died from the fire**! (Not from her injuries as her death certificate stated.) Her injuries may have been severe but we will never know if she could have survived them. *Selah.* I'm OK with this news, it was my worse case scenario and You prepared me for it back in February. *Her flesh melted off of her body according to one witness' account.*

Comfort me Lord, as I continue to tell myself that God still is in control. He knows what He is doing! This **will turn out** as Romans 8:28 for me and that I am on my way to TOTAL RESTORATION! In the NAME OF JESUS! Lord! GOD! *I expect to receive* **DOUBLE FOR ALL MY TROUBLE!**

Lord, Lord, Lord, Your Father knows what I am going through because You, His child Jesus, died a horrible death as well on the cross. Help me Holy Ghost!

Thank You for having Your angels encamped all around me. Thank You for being a fence all around me everyday, ever since half my family died and one was rescued from the fire. Kevin and Nne were consumed by the fire! Mmi was rescued from the fire! I was dropped into a spiritual fiery furnace when this happened! I feel that when they came out of the fire that night, I went in and I have had to stand and after I have done all I know to do, I continue to stand.

I pray for *supernatural* emotional healing and recovery from this trial. I want to come out of this looking like I have **NOT** been in this emotional train wreck! I want the only way that you would know it was if I told you my testimony about it! I remember being told by one of the ladies at the last retreat that I am *bearing* the weight, but not *wearing* the weight of this trial. Amen and Hallelujah! That's all **<u>You</u>**!

5/26/02

Lord,

Today was supposed to be Kevin's Second Year Anniversary Day Celebration as the church's Pastor. The church leaders didn't go through with their promised plans of recognition for him and I am really disappointed by that. I remember our conversation on why he chose this weekend to celebrate his Pastor's Anniversary instead of last weekend. It was because he would have Monday, Memorial Day, off to recuperate from the long Sunday. Now he's recuperating *forever!*

I had a birthday party in his honor on yesterday with family (my sisters came back to town) along with some of the church members. It was beautiful, well attended and *I still felt alone*, even with a house full of people. I missed Kevin and Nne again. The birthday parties for them don't make up for their absence. *I miss going to the hotel for your birthday weekend, Kevin. I miss you, Kevin, I really do miss you! I remember (us) on weekends like this and I miss you!*

5/27/02

Lord,

I'm better today. I slept most of the day, until 12:30P.M., this afternoon, while Charlotta watched Miriam who is napping now. It's just the three of us now. Jeanette and my nephew Earl have gone back to New Orleans.

I still miss you, Kevin, I really do! *I dreamt that you came back to kiss my juicy lips for your birthday!* I want it to be true but I know better. I don't want any visits from the dead and I don't want to entertain demons. So how do I feel your embrace without you being here? How do I feel your kisses without your presence? Am I reminiscing or hallucinating? What is it that I feel when I am sleeping and definitely sense a touch? Have you supernaturally come from your dimension back to mine? Why has Miriam been calling out

Daddy for the past two weeks? Why has she been calling for Nne this week? What's going on? You know I won't entertain the notion that you are trying to visit me, so you're visiting Mmi instead and she's announcing your presence to me?

Every time I sit at the table I remember you and Naomi. Every time I look at your wedding ring on my finger I remember you and our 12 years together. It was this weekend 13 years ago that you realized that God was directing you to marry me and you submitted to His counsel and followed through and asked me. And the rest, as they say, is history! I'm remembering all of this, not just your birthday and I long to be with you.

Only you and I know the bonding that occurred spiritually that weekend when I went to San Antonio and you *"panted"* for my return to Houston so that you could ask me to marry you (without a ring) and I accepted. You wanted your wife to be revealed to you by your birthday. I wanted my husband to be revealed to me by Memorial Day and that year, 13 years ago, the dates were the same! *God came through for both of us in our prayer petitions.* We were yoked together that weekend and still are! ***Selah!***

As I reflect back today on the accident, I had a sinking feeling on January 31, 2002 when I got off from work at 4:00 P.M. I almost called Kevin to tell him that I would pick up the girls from school, but my spirit would not allow me to. I came home instead and did Bible study while I waited for him to come home. I fell asleep at 5:20 P.M. after doing Bible study but again I had a sinking feeling and wanted to call Kevin but I wasn't allowed to so I fell asleep instead. While I was asleep I was restless and I kept watching the clock. The pit of my stomach was turning over and I became so nauseated I woke up in a hot sweat at 5:50 P.M.

I wanted to call again but couldn't so I got up and went to look out the door because I knew you should have been home by then. I checked the time and said that gives me enough time to get dinner on the table and I'll call while I'm doing that. I called but received no answer. That was odd, I thought, because you always kept your phone with you. I redialed again and turned on the TV to see if there was an accident that could be delaying you. There was a lead in story on the 6:00 P.M. news of an auto and train collision. My stomach ached as I continued to dial your cell number because if I could hear your voice over the phone then you were safe!

No answer!

My heart beats fast as I continue to redial your number while waiting for the news report on the accident.

No answer, again!

My heart beats faster as I placed the food on the table anticipating the upcoming news report!

We are on a church family fast and I'm waiting for all of us to get home to break the fast together as a family at our evening meal. Naomi can't wait to eat the turkey necks and greens because her braces were tightened two days earlier and she thinks she can chew the meat today. (She's had eggs and grits for dinner the last two nights.) I place her plate at her usual seat with the meat already picked from the bone to help her out with the braces. Kevin's plate is at his seat and my plate and Mmi's are in their places.

I'm watching the news and the lead in story says that a middle-age man and his teen-age daughter died as their car caught on fire after being hit by a train. My heart sinks as I immediately begin to pray for the family of the accident.

I'm still trying to reach Kevin by phone to see where he is in the traffic due to the accident I just learned about on TV. I call the girls' school to see what time Kevin signed them out and Ms. Taylor, the school's director, reported it was at 5:20 P.M. My heart pounds really fast now because I'm panicking. Still no answer on your cell phone! You checked the girls out of school by 5:20 P.M. The accident happened at 5:30 P.M. according to the news. I don't believe it's you all because they refer to the man as being middle-aged, with a teenage daughter and no mention of an infant so I don't believe it's my family. I tried calling you again and received no answer on your cell phone.

Then there was an update on the news with a live report from the scene. They say that an infant girl, around 1 year old, was rescued from the vehicle before it blew up and caught on fire and she was at the hospital in critical condition. What?!

My ears couldn't believe what I just heard!

Kevin was not middle-aged! Naomi was only <u>10</u> years old! Where did they get the information of the ages for the victims from? Was that you and Naomi they were saying was <u>*already dead*</u> on the 6:00 P.M. news? <u>No way</u>!! I tried calling you again on your cell phone and still no answer!

I watched the live pictures on TV and saw the back of <u>*my SUV*</u> and recognized the *"God Is Awesome"* frame on the rear license plate and realized that all this time I've been waiting for you all and praying for the family from the news report, it was <u>US</u>!

YOU ALL WERE DEAD when I awoke from my nap at 5:50 P.M! You were DEAD when I watched the 6:00 P.M. news! And you were DEAD as I tried to call you (finally allowed to) by phone!

WE – WERE – THE – FAMILY – I – WAS – PRAYING – FOR !!

I began to shake uncontrollably and I became physically weak as I walked to the TV to touch the screen and absorb that the burnt out vehicle I was seeing had you and Naomi's bodies in them. Miriam was in ER in critical condition at a hospital and I-I-I-I-I-I-I-sssshhhhuuuutttt down! I shut down. I shut down, emotionally! I can't absorb any more information!

I began to cry, fuss and scream at God for drafting me to this assignment! How dare HE sign me up for this special assignment without asking me? I didn't want this testimony! Not after Dad and Mom's deaths because of an auto accident 16 & 11 years ago! How could God do this to me again? What is HE trying to prove? Why, with the growing ministry Kevin and I had going on at the church did God choose to take him so suddenly? And Naomi? So young? What do I do now? <u>What now</u>?!

I sat in the floor and asked this question over and over again. What now? What now? What now? As I questioned God, I got up and paced the floor. I turned off the TV and shook my head as I trembled at the news. I'm widowed, with one child lost and one holding on for dear life according to the news reports. I couldn't believe that I WAS THE FAMILY IN THE NEWS! As I rehearsed this tragedy in my mind, I heard the doorbell ring. I looked through the peephole and I saw a Missouri City Police Officer at the door. I turned away from the door without opening it. I begin to cry out loud, *"Lord, if he's at my door then it's really true and THAT IS MY FAMILY on the news!"*

I hear him banging on my door to let him in. I tell him I can't open the door to allow him *to give me* the BAD NEWS! He says I need to open the door so he could either come in or help me, I can't remember what he said. I opened the door crying and he asked me, "Do you know already?" and I told him, "YES! I saw it on the news and recognized my SUV!" He yelled, "What? Why did they put it on the news already when I didn't have a chance to tell the family?" (*My sentiments exactly!*)

He asked to use the phone and I gave it to him and I turned back on the TV to show him the live reports about the accident. He turned it off or I did, I don't remember who did, and he told me to get dressed (because I had on my housecoat for the evening) to go to the hospital to see about Miriam. I told him *I wasn't going to the hospital to find out that Miriam didn't make it either* because they said that the baby was in critical condition.

I asked that he call the hospital to get an update and based on the news I would go to the hospital. He said, *"No, I needed to go see about the baby."* I told him if he drove me I would go. He said he couldn't drive me and he needed someone's name and telephone number to call them to come and be with me. *My mind went back to 1986 when my family had a car accident on their way here to visit me for the first time when I first moved to Houston 17 years ago.* My mind was still *"there"* and I told him I didn't know anybody here because I was new to Houston and had recently moved down here. *I was all alone – AGAIN – just like when I got the news about Dad, Mom, and my sisters' car accident and I couldn't remember anything or anybody.* I tried to share these thoughts with the officer, although he may have thought I was rambling on and on, because I needed someone to understand the impact of this devastating news to me! I needed

"My #1 Is Still My #1!"

someone who connected with me! This testimony was too much for *ME* - one person – to absorb!

My Dad, Mom, and sisters were in a tragic car accident on May 16, 1986. Dad died on impact, Mom suffered severe injuries that she subsequently died from five years later and Charlotta and Jeanette were the only ones to survive. Today, January 31, 2002, Kevin, Naomi, and Miriam were in a tragic car accident. Kevin died on impact, Nne died later on from being trapped inside the mangled car and Miriam alone survived!! And this tragedy has happened to *ME! ME! ME!* 17 years apart but both of my families in automobile accidents!! What?! No way! This CANNOT be happening again!!! *Say it isn't so!!! Say it isn't so!!!*

This makes me *not want to even drive* anymore! I tried to share this dichotomy with the officer but he *wasn't* getting it! He finally reached my church's musician on the phone and she came over to be with me along with two neighbors, *I didn't know very well.* Kevin knew every one in the neighborhood. I only saw them in passing.

I was all alone – AGAIN - even with people around me!

I said a quick prayer in my heart, "God, if You still love me *please* spare Miriam and not allow me to be *all alone* - AGAIN!" Then I got dressed, still praying silently to myself the whole time. I remembered I had put the police officer out of my house because he was fumbling for words and was of no use to me because I really needed a prayer partner. I called him back into the house, took my phone away from him and told him he could leave because the three ladies in the house with me would get me to the hospital. He left.

I asked the neighbors if they were Christians and could they pray with me for my daughter's life and health because I was afraid to go to the hospital to see about Miriam. They said they were Christians and came in agreement with me in prayer that Miriam would live and *not die!* I felt a leap in my spirit but dared not to speak of it for fear that I may be wrong and just like earlier that day I would find out that it wasn't good news for me.

I tried to figure out how to tell my sisters what had happened. I had just come back from visiting them in New Orleans last week for Jeanette's kidney donor transplant operation and Charlotta was at Jeanette's house helping her to recuperate from the surgery. I just called Jeanette's house and angrily told them what had happened to Kevin, Nne, and Mmi. They cried and couldn't believe the news and said they were on their way to Houston to come see about me. <u>Yes</u>! I would NOT be alone! *My sisters were on their way to come see about ME!*

I left for the hospital with our church musician, Sister Mincey, who lived near us and left the neighbors at my house to pick up around there and to answer the phone for me. I prayed all the way to the hospital that God would accept my prayer and leave me Miriam. When we got to the hospital I identified myself to ER and they scared me even more by their reluctance to look me in the eye or tell me my baby's status. All they said was for me *"to wait for the hospital director and he'll escort you to see your daughter."* He was dressed in a business suit and didn't say one word to me besides *"Follow me."* My heart sank again, because no one was talking to me and I feared the worse. When we arrived at Miriam's room I couldn't walk through the door. I sent Sister Mincey in to survey the situation for me and report back to me. After she went in and looked things over, she said it was OK for me to go in.

I walked in and saw Mmi being rocked by a male nurse with monitors all over her chest down to her toes. SHE LOOKED LIKE HELL, but she was *alive*!! Hallelujah! She was blistered on her forehead and feet and still blanketed in soot from the fire. She had burns on her right ear, nose and cheek and all of her hair was singed and scorched off to their roots. She made it through the fire *and* she recognized me as her Mommy! She reached for me and I reached for her and I couldn't believe that <u>God still loved me</u>! As far as I was concerned, Miriam only had cosmetic burns, could still recognize me as her Mommy, and WANTED ME to hold her! God still loved me - *through her! He heard my prayers and answered me!* <u>YEAH</u>!

I gave her back to the male nurse and I began to praise and thank the Lord for answering my prayer by blessing me with somebody to start over with. I knew I could do nothing for Kevin and Naomi. They were already gone, but Miriam was alive and I was here for her, Hallelujah! The hospital personnel asked me if I knew what had happened to the rest of my family. I told them, *"yes,"* and they asked me if I needed a sedative (shot) I told them, *"no!"* I just hugged and kissed on Miriam and I was in another world. Kevin and Naomi were together, sadly, and Mmi and I were together, thankfully.

So many people started arriving at the hospital that their faces are a blur to me now. I do remember calling my sister-in-law, Charolette's cell number and telling her while she was at work but that's the last thing I remember. I also tried to call my mother-in-law, Laverne, but she had turned her phone off and I couldn't reach her, but she and everyone else in Kevin's family still made it out to the hospital. I do recall that most of the church family came out, along with our friends and associates. I also remember seeing my mentor and prayer partner, Mia Wright, who came there to be with me.

There was prayer, intercession, tears, shock, and disbelief among us. I was thinking, *"What now, Lord?"* It's just me and Miriam, *what now, Lord?* While I was thinking to myself, I had an out of body experience with me hovering over everybody as they arrived there at the hospital. Then my heart began pounding hard and fast again. It almost pounded out of my chest. I began to hyperventilate because I needed air. I couldn't breath. The hospital people tried to help me but I wouldn't let them. I only thought I needed some water because my mouth was so dry!

More police officers came by the hospital to tell me about the car accident and that Naomi was alive in the fire! <u>What</u>?! I fainted! When I came to they had put me on Miriam's bed and had given me oxygen and a shot in the arm. The hospital wanted to keep me overnight, but I refused.

I wanted to choke the life out of the police officer who told me that Nne was alive when the fire consumed her! How insensitive can you be? I was already overcome by the news of their deaths and *she had to tell me* that my daughter was alive when she burned to death?! I didn't need to know that!! Help me, Holy Ghost, Help me Jesus! I went for her throat for being such an idiot. I only wanted to know that they didn't suffer and she took that away from me by telling me that about Nne. That police officer even admitted that she had children of her own yet and still she was so insensitive with giving me the news about *my child!* Help me, Holy Ghost!! I wanted to run away, run up to the scene of the accident to see for myself, but I knew better than to try to see for myself. Thank You for keeping me from myself!!

Lord, Lord, Lord, what now?! I'm left with a baby to raise alone!! Please help me!! I begin to shut down again emotionally because this is too much for me to humanly process. The Holy Ghost takes over me and I'm on automatic pilot now…

Lord, what *IS* my destiny? All of this that I am experiencing is because of the divine purpose that You've designed me for, right, so what is it? I want to press in to receive it. *The time is now, RIGHT!?* So let's get to it!! You've protected me and kept me for Your purpose. You've preserved me in my right mind with Romans 8:28 to sustain me. What would You have me to do? Wasn't I doing it before? How can I *better serve You* as a widow and single mom? What have You prophesied over me? Kevin and Naomi weren't a part of Your plan for me, only Miriam?

So, here I am, with angels encamped all around me, ready to know. ***What Now?***

5/29/02

Lord,
Today is Kevin's 39th birthday and he isn't here! He's with You! He died so young! It's hard to be here without him on his birthday! But I'm making it through, I brought Miriam to work with me today and she wore me out! We played around the house this evening and wore ourselves out and went to bed early tonight.

I guess I'm handling his birthday *"well"* I don't know what that is, nor what it means when others say it.

Last night was Naomi's end of the school year Awards Program and it was very difficult for me. My heart was heavy with sorrow and grief over her absence at her own awards program. I wanted to be there, but it was bittersweet for me. It was great to see her classmates, but saddening for me to see them without her. Laverne and Miriam attended the ceremony with me and the parents, staff, and students were patient with me as I cried silently while receiving a presentation from the school on behalf of Nne. I asked them to give me honorary certificates of the awards Nne would have earned and they agreed to do it. Light Christian Academy has been really great in recognizing Naomi and not forgetting my daughter. **Praise the Lord!!**

I wonder why it's so hard for our own church to remember Kevin and recognize him as being a part of their lives.

JUNE

6/2/02

Lord,
 I made it through this *emotionally difficult* past week! Yeah!! Hallelujah!!

    Tuesday, 5/28/02 - Nne's School Awards Program
    Wednesday, 5/29/02 - Kevin's Birthday
    Thursday, 5/30/02 - Nne's Honorary Awards given to me, Dad's
                          Birthday
    Saturday, 6/1/02 - Kevin's youngest brother, Frank's Wedding
    Sunday, 6/2/02 - Charlotta/Mom's Birthday

It was a **VERY FULL** week and now it's the night time going into my last week of work - YEAH! I made it through several steps on my journey through grief recovery! My return back to work, significant *"firsts"* without Kevin/Nne like Mother's Day, Birthdays, Awards Days, Weddings, Family Reunions, etc. all have gone on even with Kevin and Nne being gone. People are getting married, having babies, buying houses, and carrying on with their lives even while I struggle to adjust to life as a single mother. I have two significant losses here that I live with daily. I pout, stomp in the ground, and holler *"Hey you people looky here, I am alone now – I am only sane for Miriam, who is too young to console me - and you all are going on like no one has died! Looky here, looky here! I'm longing for my family to be complete again and you all are moving* *on with your lives - what gives?"* Life is going full speed ahead and too fast for me! Life needs to slow down and allow me to catch up! I feel left behind, running behind a new life trying to catch up and on to the "train" that pulled out and left me and Miriam behind!

Sometimes, I feel like the unseen world penetrates into this world and touches me and tries to comfort me when I am lonely. Is it angels? I know Kevin/Nne can't come back, so is it the angels You, God, have encamped all around me that move in this realm to protect me from hurt, harm, and danger? Like today for instance, when I fell backwards off the couch I was standing on and I felt *"something"* **break my fall so that I wouldn't hurt myself. I know no one was physically there but I felt some hands holding me up until I could stand up straight from the fall. What gives? Other times I have felt a physical embrace when no one else was there to hold me...**

I do miss Kevin this time of the year, it's time for our love-a-thon and he's not here to participate. *Thank You Lord, for keeping me!* It's as if *all sexual desire* has been *turned off* since the accident and I'm not interested in sex at all! *Thank You Lord, for keeping me!!*

Frank's wedding yesterday was very difficult for me to witness, knowing that Kevin would have **loved to have married his brother and his bride.** He counseled Frank so much when he was alive and to not be present at his wedding was like Kevin being short changed. There never would have been a good time for him to die. There always would have been an occasion to celebrate! Thank You for giving me the phrase, *"I'll be alright even though it ain't alright right now. It will get better."* That phrase carried me through the wedding and reception and it answered a lot of inquiring minds as well.

I visited Nate Johnson's (a Pastor friend of Kevin's) church today and realized from his sermon that my home church has been my *"Rachel"* and other ministries have been my *"Leah."* I need to wake up and appreciate the other ministries and quit running after the hope that my home church will finally realize the jewels they had in me and Kevin and show appreciation for us. They may never wake up, and I <u>*must-needs*</u> to move on. Help me Lord to realize that *"their trash" will be <u>another</u> ministry's treasure* in due season!

Help me Holy Ghost and Help Me God! *You alone know <u>how hard</u> this trial is for me!*

6/5/02

Lord,
    I realized through working in my anger workbook that my disappointment over Your not stopping the accident was really a shade of <u>ANGER</u>! You had the power to stop the accident from happening and ***You didn't!!*** Now I am a widow with a baby to raise all alone! Why didn't our daily prayers for safety and protection cover them? Why didn't Kevin stay behind the damn railroad arms? Why did he have to cross the tracks? Why did my daughter have to burn alive to death? ***Why, why, why?!***
    You alone know the answer - ***are You willing to share?*** Am I ready to know? How does this work for my good? (Romans 8:28) We had a good family life, and then in a moment on 1/31/02 it all vanished. I had a good husband, a godly husband and an obedient child - both are gone from me now! Kevin made an error in judgment that cost him his life and our daughter's. One reckless decision to go across the tracks even though the arms were down and now he's home with You and Miriam and I are left behind. I thank You that Miriam is here with me, but I still lament over the loss of my husband and daughter. I miss them!
    The summer is here when we used to plan activities and trips as a family, now it's only me and Miriam. No summer reading clubs for Nne, no lying around the house lazily, sleeping in and letting Nne watch Mmi. No spooning together in bed for Kevin and me while Nne tries her hand at frying eggs as breakfast for all of us. *No memories to create of "The Dickey Family's summer of 2002."*
    Last summer, 2001, was the first and only summer the four of us were all together. We went to New Orleans for vacation last June before Tropical Storm Allison hit Houston and we played like "tourists" per Nne's request. We visited the Aquarium and stayed at a hotel, and we visited a local church we usually watched on TV from Houston. We were even filmed while there and later saw ourselves on TV at the church in a later broadcast!

We had a great time together last summer in our hotel loft. Nne had upstairs to herself and we had downstairs with a fridge and microwave. It was great! We came back to Houston and relaxed the whole summer. We were off together for the first time and had saved up money to make it through summer without feeling strapped financially. We had a fabulous summer last year even as I realized, in hindsight, that it was to be our last one together as a family. We purchased two new vehicles one in June, the other in July. We named them Favor and More Favor, Kevin and Naomi died in "More Favor." *Can it get any more ironic than that?*

6/8/02

Lord,

I go back and forth. Sometimes I can wait for the Romans 8:28 in my experience and at other times I don't even know what You're doing and wonder why I should even wait on Romans 8:28. I'm confused at times, and at others I can see with my spiritual eyes. I've been praying for myself to have strength to make it through the day and other days I just want to be left alone!

6/10/02

Lord,

Please reconcile with me this debate of Premature Death vs. God's Sovereignty.

Did Kevin and Naomi die prematurely as an attack of the devil against my faith? Or was their time still in Your hands? **Help me to reconcile this!** In my head, I rationalize that Kevin/Nne were so young and had so much more to live for. In my heart, I believe You are in control, was in control on 1/31/02 and allowed this for Your own reason. But I still ask, *"Couldn't they have stayed here a little while longer?"*

SPIRITUAL WARFARE!! SPIRITUAL WARFARE!!

I'm on the battlefield for my Lord! Thank You for keeping me, Lord!! This is for sure a test of my character. I pray I am doing well over all. People say that I am looking *"well"* (*whatever that means*), how am I supposed to look? **If You are God in my life - shouldn't I *look* (strong) like You?** Shouldn't I be able to endure this? Please God, please, continue to strengthen me in this test of my faith!

6/11/02

Lord,

It is so-o-o hard for me to comprehend the fact that Kevin and Naomi are really gone! They are not just away and will return shortly, walking through that front door after a four month absence. I used to spend so much time alone with Miriam and then they would come home to give me a break from care-giving. But they haven't taken their shift in four months and I am carrying the load all alone. Miriam is a challenge, full of energy and she reminds me of myself before the stress of this trial.

Today I learned from the coroner's report that Naomi was burned to a crisp. There was no flesh left on her bones, no internal organs, nothing but charred bones. She was seated right above where the gas tank exploded so she was in direct line of the fire. She melted just like the eyewitnesses' stated. Kevin had some skin left on his body according to the coroner's report. He wasn't directly above the gas tank like Nne was. But it's pretty clear that they both burned, he after dying on impact from the train collision and she because of the explosion. She was in and out of consciousness until she was killed by the fire.

HOW HORRIBLE!! HORRIBLE!! HORRIBLE!! HORRIBLE!!

For me to even think that she knew what was happening to her and couldn't be rescued is torture! I can't even think about it without shutting down emotionally, it's too much to fathom. She saw them save Miriam but they couldn't save her because she was trapped by the twisted metal. **How awful!!** Kevin was gone by the time the passersby got to the car, perhaps his soul and spirit lingered (*hovered over the vehicle*) to wait for Naomi to join him on that great chariot to Glory. It just *hurts so much* to be left behind on this side of heaven without my number one and number two cheerleaders, especially after learning these gory details.

GGGGGGGGGGO-O-O-O-O-O-D-D-D-D!!

Why didn't You prevent this accident?
Why did they have to die so horribly?
What was the purpose of their manner of death?
How does this fit into your Romans 8:28 for me?

Please, please, please – <u>*COMFORT ME*</u>*!!* **JESUS! JESUS! JESUS! JESUS! JESUS!**

6/12/02

Lord,
Delayed grieving is the pits!

 I have many things that need to be done around the house and no one around to help me! Everyone has moved on and gone on and *now I really need them!* I can't do anything with Miriam home because she demands so much of my attention. I may have an overly ambitious *"to do"* list for my five weeks off for summer vacation. I want to:

  1. Clean out receipt drawer and file papers
  2. Clean out garage/throw away some items/store other things properly
  3. Get blinds for the windows in the back of the house
  4. Install the water softener
  5. Get reliable maid service in place for Mmi and me
  6. Upgrade the computer
  7. Get more bookshelves in the study

8. Get spa supplies replaced for the Jacuzzi
9. Get carpet cleaned
10. Buy new furniture for the bedroom
11. Buy new dining room set and
12. Buy a wall unit for the video tapes

I spelled P-A-I-N R-E-L-I-E-F using all of my coping strategies today. I cooked meals (needlessly), I ate ice cream, I wrote in my journal, and I cried. I did all of this, one after the other as well as prayed positive faith confessions for grief recovery and even walked for exercise, and **I am still anxious!** I need to calm down! I do remember having an Rx for Xanax to help me out that I usually take as my last resort...

When I try to process in my mind the cause of death for Naomi, my first-born, I get forgetful, absentminded, and impatient and I lose my train of thought... What else am I suppose to be doing? I need to keep my schedule updated. I am supposed to be going to lunch with somebody tomorrow...

Reading through the lawsuit's discovery questions really agitated and irritated me today. I have to meet with the lawyers again on Friday to answer questions for the lawsuit against the railroad company and the written questions made me irritated and anxious.

Why am I here?

Why has life's circumstances led me to this place in life?

I am forced to cope with the reality that Nne/Kevin died tragically and *You, God, did not prevent it* for whatever reason! Lord, please keep my mind stayed on You. Tonight, I will read the Scriptures until I fall asleep. Please, give me a restful, peaceful sleep. Lord, also allow Miriam to sleep through the night to help me deal with my sleep deprivation during this summer vacation, Amen!

6/13/02

Lord,

Today was a better day for me emotionally. I had two good therapy sessions that helped me **to see me** in this trial. It opened up my wounds and exposed me for who I am right now on the inside. I

"My #1 Is Still My #1!"

am a scared woman child wondering who is left on this earth to love me now – presently! Kevin loved me with Agape, Phileo and Eros love. Naomi loved me unconditionally because I was her mother. Now I'm missing out on these intimate love relationships. *I truly am!*

What I know for sure is that Kevin and Nne were my number one and number two cheerleaders, and NOBODY can take that away from me!

6/15/02

Lord,

When I think about how the church leadership *used* Kevin and me, I get angry all over again! I think, "They never loved *us*! They loved *what we did* for the church." It is very hurtful to me to realize that they never invested themselves emotionally into us and were only along for the ride, not equally participating in building up our relationship, but only in it to take what we had to give!

As I was showering today, I began to think about it differently. I thought who were we really serving, them or You, Lord? Undeniably, You! *You were our Lord* and not that church! Who were we used by, then? Unequivocally, *You!* What was the purpose of our season over there? *To show them Your love for them through us? I don't know, I'm only guessing.* I know they had *no love* to offer us. Kevin said we had to agape love them back to spiritual wholeness because of their brokenness.

Kevin and I did agape love them with the love of the Lord, and now we're out of there! What now, Lord? **Kevin is DEAD!** I am still here and now *I am mad at them*! After all that agape love we showed them by example they still didn't get it! Was our time wasted? Could we have done better elsewhere? Why can't those ingrates show me love? Why are they so emotionally and spiritually retarded, Lord? Will they ever truly become saved? And why did I have to go through all of this hell and rejection at my church home after already losing my husband and daughter? Why? Why? Why, Lord? What now, Lord, what now? I am wandering through a spiritually barren wilderness and I don't like this feeling of being *"spiritually homeless"* in regards to a church home.

Please continue to guide me and protect me as I walk behind You in the footprints in the sand that You have left for me. *The song, "Order my steps in Your Word, Dear Lord!" written by Glen Bruleigh continues to sing in my heart.*

6/17/02

Thank You, Lord for ordering my steps on tonight!

I needed for You to release me from the anger and hatred I was feeling towards the church leadership team and their new Pastor for betraying me. You set me up for deliverance at the Fountain of Praise (Mia's church) tonight and you had Yolande there *to preach to me and my situation.* Hallelujah! I was bound up with anger, bitterness and whatever else travels with those demons and I was not even able to pray for myself. I knew ***I had to get to where You could meet me and my needs*** because I couldn't even get a prayer through. At the Fountain of Praise, I met You after the crowd had left. You met me, ministered to me and healed me (again)! I wanted this root of bitterness to come up and out of me. I wanted the toxic poison of anger to come up and out, so that I could move on.

Praise and Worship was the perfect combination and solution to driving the toxic poisons out of my system. It worked (**AGAIN**)! I can't believe how often I get entangled and caught up in the negative emotions that accompany the whole church drama. I wanted to be released from my anger, hurt, pain and bitterness and I felt that on tonight I got that release. After being slain in the Spirit, I came up off the floor dancing before You in worship, adoration and thanksgiving. Hallelujah for deliverance yet again!

I LOVE YOU, JESUS! I WORSHIP AND ADORE YOU! I JUST WANT TO TELL YOU, THAT I LOVE YOU - MORE THAN ANYTHING! (An anointed song by Lamar Campbell that sings in my heart)

I know You're not trying to kill me but to prune me and when I get through, I will come forth as pure gold!! (1 Peter 1:7, NKJV) Hallelujah! Continue to show me Your love in this process through those vessels that make themselves available to YOU for Me! I can feel Your anointing on me again, thank You!!

6/22/02

Lord,

When You showed Joseph he would be ruler over Egypt You didn't show him the years in between his dream at 17 years old and his promotion to become second to Pharaoh at age 30. (Genesis 37-41) In those in between years Joseph experienced family rejection, enslavement, incarceration, **and then promotion.** When I saw in a vision where You would elevate me to become *a nationally recognized writer and teacher who would testify about You to the nations* I didn't see my own in between years just like Joseph.

I thought I had enough testimonies to write about from my childhood (alcoholic father), young adulthood (drugged and date raped, Dad's death, Mom's death), young married wife (with a sickly daughter, Naomi, and under employed spouse) and being a Pastor's wife (enough said!). Now I have widowhood and the loss of a child to add to my spiritual teachings and writings. My Lord, my God, I thought I had enough life experiences to draw from and then You allowed more sorrow and sadness to come to me on 1/31/02.

Again, I have no idea what You're preparing me for but I trust that it will all work together for my good and You will fit it all together for me in due season. *My gift IS ABOUT to be OPENED* and *You have loosed me* in this dispensation for such a time as this! Lord, continue to keep me safe in Your arms, to order my steps to the places You have ordained for me, and to recognize Your Love for me when shown through Your willing vessels!

Lord, I cannot reconcile (<u>*again!*</u>) that Kevin made a judgment that cost him his life and Naomi's! He chose to follow behind the other drivers who made it around the railroad arms safely even though the arms were down. He thought it would be safe for him to also go around the arms (*I still can't believe he made that decision*) and he was hit by a train he didn't see coming. He died immediately. Nne afterwards. Mmi alone was rescued to be here with me. *"Oh, How I Love Jesus! Oh, How I Love Jesus!*

"My #1 Is Still My #1!"

Oh, How I Love Jesus, because He first Loved Me!" (The Baptist Hymnal song written by Fredrick Whitfield that distracts me from this pain in my heart)

6/23/02

Lord,

I know what Your love feels like because I experienced it through Kevin during our marriage over the past 12 years! He loved me with a God type of love, unconditionally, unequivocally and absolutely! I loved him immensely and miss our day-to-day boring experiences and intimate conversations. I don't think I ever would have been ready for this chapter in my life to come to an end. I do love You, God, but having someone on this side of heaven to help the flesh cope with this pilgrim's journey makes the trip easier. I truly enjoyed being married to Kevin and I thank You for yoking us up together over 12 years ago.

*I can't believe that **I'm back on the "market"** (whatever that means) as a result of this tragic experience. How in the world can I move forward after this type of tragedy?*

I want Miriam to know the love of a Daddy through daily interactions with a father figure. I want a mature man of God who knows Your will for his life and is actively pursuing it!! Anyone coming after Kevin as a husband and father would have a tough act to follow. He left huge shoes to fill and the next fellow will have to come on with it spiritually *if he even thinks about stepping to me and Miriam!* I pray the new man can handle a mature woman of God (me) and her baby of destiny and purpose (Miriam).

I know the plans You have for me are to prosper me and not to harm me, plans to give me hope and a future. (Jeremiah 29:11)

I have called upon You and I have come to You (to You) and have prayed to You and I have listened for You to respond. I have sought You and I have sought You with my whole heart. *You are a rewarder of those who <u>diligently</u> seek You. (Hebrews11:6, NKJV) Selah.*

Lord, I <u>desperately</u> want to know what the next step in Your will for my life is!

I earnestly desire wisdom and direction in the way I should go!

6/26/02

Lord,

I've been thinking if our lives are a vapor that evaporates after a short time (like our breath when it's cold) then Kevin and Nne's lives were like short vapors. Kevin's vapor lasted 38 seconds because he was only 38years old. Nne's vapor lasted 10 seconds for her 10 years of life. Both of their lives were very short vapors when considered from Your perspective. When I rise above my circumstances and try to see things from Your perspective, it eases my pain. It causes me to be grateful for the short time we had together for it was longer than our breath which evaporates quickly in the cold air here on earth. Thanks for a different (Your) perspective, which really helped!

I went to the crematory on Tuesday (*I had to*) to see their inventory records and to see the process a body goes through in cremation. I saw in their records that Kevin weighed in at 275 lbs, he lost more than 65 lbs in the car fire. Naomi weighed in at 75 lbs, and she lost 35 lbs in the car fire. They were reduced to 11 lbs, 6oz of ashes for Kevin and 5 lbs, 5oz of ashes for Nne. ***It is really true! The crematory has dated records of their cremation!***

THEY ARE REALLY GONE and the ashes I possess are all I have of their remains!

· I plan on spreading their ashes and then have only their urns to memorialize their deaths. Their spirits are still here with me, but I miss being able to hold them physically. I need to reconcile that they cannot be held by me on this side, anymore. Miriam is all I have to hold on to from mine and Kevin's union and my only evidence that I really was married before and it's not all in my imagination.

I still can't believe this has happened to me! I keep thinking that the joke would be on me and they will return and say *"Gotcha!"*

I would reply that they really had me going for close to five months and we will laugh, cry, punch each other in the arm and it will all be over! Then I remember, intellectually I know, that my *new reality* is true and this is it. I remember that I have a new life now! And I have to get on with it and stop reminiscing! But how do I do that when I still want to feel the hugs of my daughter and husband again!

This summer without them is full of mind numbing activity with Miriam but *I still know they are missing!* I miss hanging out lazily for the summer with them and lounging around the house. I miss Nne being in the summer reading club through the library and how she couldn't wait for Vacation Bible School at Windsor Village United Methodist Church (WVUMC) to start because *she absolutely loved* **their children's church**. She grew up spiritually at that church along with the Godly influence and great parenting from her own Mommy and Daddy! ☺

How could Kevin think I would be all right without him? Didn't he know I would go through changes? How come people like to overlook the spiritual labor one has to go through in order to be spiritually strong? They figure, *"Oh, you're a strong Christian and you will make it through your test or trial!"* **but they fail to realize that the process** *"strong"* **people go through is the same as what other folks have to go through to "come through" the trial. We may endure it better, but it's a test and trial for us just the same!**

Don't trivialize our trials just because as *"strong people going through a test of our faith"* **you assume we have the emotional and spiritual tools to make it through on our own without any outside help, comfort or prayers! We feel pain! We go through things! We agonize! We question! And we want to run away from it all too! We still need the support and encouragement from others to hang in there! OK? We are still human! We just know from experience that eventually all roads for healing lead to God! We know better than to go down any other roads because the <u>FIRST</u> one that leads to Him is the right one!!** *We all will have to come to Him and go through Him! So we "strong" people go to Him <u>FIRST</u>,* **to get our day of reckoning over with and wind up staying with Him until our healing is manifested!**

***God IS* our refuge and strength, an ever-present help in time of trouble!! (Psalm 46:1) HALLELUJAH!**

Right now I feed on the Word of God like a deer pants for water. I keep going back to it, it gets/keeps my head clear, and my focus in check and **IT IS** my plumb line! God's Word is my Balm in Gilead, it soothes my broken heart, it mends it with its salve and spiritually I can see the gaping hole in my heart closing and coming back together now. I don't feel so opened up on the trauma table of ER like before when I was attending my old church. I feel the spiritual stitches of the Word of God pulling (like a magnet) my broken pieces back together and putting my heart back together again. *"Oh, How I Love Jesus, no one can tear us apart. He took my broken pieces and gave me a brand new start! Oh, How I love Jesus!"* (Refrain from the same titled song by Shirley Caesar in my heart)

Lord, I don't feel as emotionally overwhelmed by this trial anymore, I am just sad as I realize that I have Miriam to raise alone without her loving Dad. I know the benefits of having a God fearing husband and Dad in a daughter's life and I don't know what's in store for Miriam without her Daddy's influence. I pray diligently for Miriam and I ask You for wisdom, guidance, and direction in filling in the emotional gaps for her. I don't know how long this season of single parenting will be for us and I want to be emotionally prepared as a single Mom for Miriam's sake.

I do sense that at some time in the future, You will allow me to remarry. I just don't know when and to whom. I pray that whoever (he is) is seasoned as a Christian and has gone through some heartbreak of his own to truly understand where Miriam and I are coming from. I pray for a gentle spirit with an affectionate nature like her Daddy, Kevin, to show Miriam public demonstrative love. I want him to have Kevin's passion and love for God's Word and to be willing to lead by example in lifestyle, giving, praying, and integrity like he did for our family.

I guess what I'm saying is, I don't want to lose any of the spiritual and emotional ground that *Kevin and I had recovered for our own family* from each of our family's generational curses. I want someone (if You allow it) who can pick up where Kevin and I left off and not miss a beat in the rhythm of working as co-laborers for

Christ in the vineyard of the Lord. You gave me the desires of my heart exceedingly, abundantly, above all I could think to ask before when You gave me Kevin and I believe that You can do it again, *if You choose to do so*. Fine tune my order for a husband as only You know how, because the man You give me will have to go through tests and trials and grow spiritually from them like Kevin and I did. *Kevin and I were made for each other for that season of my life, what more can I say?*

Lord, God, I have a few questions for You:

What do You (God) do when Adam (Kevin) dies and leaves behind his rib Eve (me)? If she (I) was from *that* Adam's rib can she (I) be fashioned for another Adam? Or does she (I) go it alone like Anna, the prophetess, in Luke 2:36? What is Your Word for young widows in the Bible? Please direct me to it, so that I can do a Bible study on this topic and research the promises you have for me and Miriam.

WIDOWHOOD!!

I never saw this in my future! I thought me and Kevin would grow old together, watching our girls work alongside of us with their own families in the ministry.

But, Kevin chose to go around the railroad arms and took a risk that cost him his life and Naomi's. So now, that chapter of my life's book has ended and I'm in transition awaiting my next assignment.

I'm just dumbfounded at how quickly my life has changed! That in a twinkling of an eye, I have been left in an emotional wreck of which I am still recovering from! *This is simply <u>UNBELIEVABLE</u>!! My life as a mother of two wonderful girls and an adored wife of a devoted and awesome man of God <u>IS OVER</u>!!*

God, how can You possibly top that?! I had a great life, in my opinion! I know You are a forward moving God and that You do things that blow our minds. I cannot conceive in my mind of how my life could be better, but my past experiences with You have shown me that the *"BEST IS (STILL) YET TO COME!"*

Each year with You has been better than the year before, even the bitter years due to deaths, grief and sorrows. I've come back spiritually each time before with a vengeance and Satan had to look out because I was kicking devil butts and taking names later. I see the same in this experience as well, but I can't quite see it coming together just yet. You still have me in the dark on this one. It's still unfolding with many twists and turns along with multiple variables that are coming into play to determine the final outcome.

I still trust You, God, with the details of my life! My life is still in YOUR hands!

You have kept my mind stayed on You. The Holy Ghost has coached me through some tough days in this grief recovery journey and I'm feeling stronger with each emotional hurdle I make it over. My emotional wounds are not gaping open anymore. Hallelujah! They are still in bandages and in some places I'm still broken, but I'm treating them with *Your prescription, Your Word, taken as often as needed!*

I'll be alright as long as I continue to convalesce in Your Word, keep Godly counsel, and maintain intimacy with You through prayer, meditation, and stillness before You!!

God *is* my Jehovah Rapha!

He makes my bitter experiences sweet! I am relying on that promise as my *"carrot"* through this difficult experience. **God has got to work Romans 8:28 out in this experience! I am confident of** *that one thing! It WILL happen! I just have to keep on believing it!!*

I'm encouraged in my spirit since I poured out my soul to You in writing tonight! I've purged myself of everything toxic yet again! Selah!

JULY

7/9/02

Lord,

In my quiet time, You have counseled me to forgive the church leaders at my former church and I have stopped fighting the promptings. I can sincerely say that I have moved toward forgiveness of the church leadership team for their offenses towards me. You reminded me that You forgave me of my offenses towards You, so I must follow Your example and I did. I have even uttered a prayer for *"Mercy on them"* because they have no idea of whom they are being subject to. Their master (Satan) is hidden even from them.

I suggested to the members that called me over the weekend that they form a prayer team and intercede for the church, leaders, and members. They said that the members are tired and weary and won't participate in prayer service anymore. Oh well, I can't make the "horses" drink the water, I'm having a hard enough time bringing the "horses" to the well.

On the flip side, I know I've been delivered from my soul ties to the old church because hearing their news of the manipulative back door schemes and deals didn't provoke me nor bother me. Although encouraged by them to join in the manipulation, I didn't even have to pray about it in order to shout, "NO!!" Some things I just know, not to even do! Thank You that I could rejoice with, and in You, and not be sucked into the drama at the old church.

You, Jehovah-God, know what You're doing! I may not know and even they may not know, but *You know*, God!! All the things that are happening over there are happening because You are allowing it for Your reasons. I'm out of the way! Hallelujah! When You move at the old church, I won't be around to blame – Amen!

Miriam is so cute! While I was praying she got down on her knees, then lay down prostrate with her head down and tickled me so I couldn't pray! She beat me to the floor as she saw me kneeling and knew my routine and jumped ahead of me saying – "Halle", for Hallelujah! She was so adorable! I knew Kevin and Naomi were looking and smiling at us, *along with You!*

My trip to New Orleans last week was exhausting! I had something going on everyday and the busyness wore me out. I thank You Lord, because I met You at several of the church and family fellowships that I attended while in New Orleans.

I want to thank You for the breakthrough I received on last Sunday, June 30, when I just shouted out all of my pain! I screamed and hollered *so much!* I was empty! I think I got it all out! I don't know, only You know for sure. The Kurt Carr song, *"The Blood Still Has Miraculous Power,"* was a Rhema Word *to* me and *for* me. The praise dancers were so anointed and their worship through dance broke the yolk of sorrow and grief in my spirit off of me. I felt like I was torn open from the top of my head to the bottom of my feet. I felt You coming down supernaturally from heaven to come and see about me! *You comforted me!* You came to check on me, before, during and after my anointed encounter in that Praise and Worship! Thank You!! Thank You!! Thank You!!

You just *kept showing up* in New Orleans everyday to comfort me. You kept me distracted (again) from remembering the last time I visited with my whole family in December 2001. Thank You, Jesus!

It's getting better for me – day by day – <u>it really is</u>!! Hallelujah!

I don't feel like I'm in the fiery furnace like I have felt before. I am beginning to feel like this fiery trial is cooling off for me. ***PRAISE THE LORD!*** I realized that all the prayer wheels have truly been turning in my direction because I feel relieved from the emotional weight of this trial.

I have solicited prayer from The Kingdom Builders Prayer Institute Team, a prayer ministry of WVUMC, as well as other ministries and they all have me on their prayer list for at least the next 30 days. I've asked everyone I know who is a prayer warrior to intercede on my behalf. I want them to keep me ever before the Lord as I seek Him for direction on the next matter in my life!

I'm still trusting, obeying, and listening for Your voice, Lord. I heard You on the drive home from New Orleans. You gave me *"Bright Educational Resources"* as a name for one of my businesses. I remember registering that name in Houston ten years ago as a DBA (doing business as) name for myself. I may finally have a use for it! That was the name I heard for me to go register again as I set myself up for promotion according to Your will and direction.

I will be obedient. You will work out the details of what we will do in the business later. Thank You, God, for being faithful, even while I struggled to hold on. **You** believed in me and trusted me to come through and still serve You while I'm going through. **You trust** me to continue to give You praise as I go through. **You trust me** to give You Glory as You lift my spirits and keep my mind stayed on You. As I concentrate on You and meditate on You, my healing bursts forth speedily – Hallelujah!

Lord, I'm still trying to recuperate from my trip to New Orleans before having to leave tomorrow for Bishop T.D. Jakes' Woman Thou Art Loosed (WTAL'02) Conference in Dallas! Please restore my body, speedily!

7/12/02

Lord God,
Thank you for leading me to the WTAL'02 Conference in Dallas, TX this past weekend. You did a marvelous thing by ordering my steps to the Potters House where *You* put me back together again! There was a supernatural exchange made in that spiritually charged atmosphere! An instant healing! A knowing of the moment I was

healed emotionally from grief! You did an **"AWESOME THING"** in less than six months! You healed my broken heart and all its pieces after my grievous experience from the 1/31/02 tragedy!! *I know it's done!* I have been feeling the spiritual sutures pulling the pieces of my heart back together in the Spirit as I had written before. But now, *I "see" spiritually by faith* that You supernaturally closed the hole in my heart and filled me with Your Joy, Peace, and Presence in that WTAL'02 Conference! I am no longer empty, but filled up to overflowing, and I'm not leaking anymore! *I can now <u>hold the anointing</u> that You have deposited in me! I can pour it out on others, <u>instead of</u> it seeping through the cracks that are in me! Hallelujah!!*

I thank you for Your supernatural timing, in that You were faithful to do what I asked of You back in February! *I asked You that if <u>I had to</u> go through this trial, please shorten the process and comfort and guide me <u>every step</u> of the way!* Hallelujah for Your faithfulness to Your Word! I knew I was healed when my thoughts went to my house and I saw myself putting away the funeral displays that I had in the living room and finally having the courage to remove Kevin's wedding ring from my hand. When I got home I did exactly what I had mentally rehearsed in my head at the conference. And the spirit of grief **did not** come over me as I removed the items that had fed my soul and my flesh these past few months.

God, You *really, really, really, really blessed me* in the meetings at the WTAL'02 Conference! You absolutely restored unto me the joy of my salvation! My Rhema Word came when one of the speakers said that *I didn't need a man* to do the supernatural things of God! That word just sank into my spirit like an anchor! I thought that I needed Kevin to do the supernatural things that God showed me in visions and dreams. You told me, as You have shown me these past five months that **You alone are my <u>SOURCE</u>!** You are my strength, not my late husband, *not even a new one*! You are going to do a new thing in me with ministry and my businesses. I won't need a natural man alongside of me to make this happen, You alone, will do it! Hallelujah!!

I regained so much confidence in myself and my calling at the WTAL '02 Conference! My heart has finally caught up with my head and they are synchronized to move forward towards my divine destiny for this season! We are all in step now - spirit, soul, and body - to move forward in You, God. I've been taught how to take control of the soulish realm and dictate from the Spirit on how my body should respond to tests, trials, temptations, and circumstances. **I choose <u>to continue</u> to operate in the Spirit and not in the flesh!**

So many of the speakers lined up with what I needed to hear spiritually and passed me along to the next one, propelling me to springboard to my next level. I planted several faith seeds at the Potter's House. I believe *I planted whole fields of seeds* that will come up and overtake me during my harvest time in *Your season and timing for me.* The anointing was very strong in one of the sessions to break spiritual strongholds and I responded by planting a sacrificial offering on behalf of my dreams for future ministries, businesses, and supernatural favor in the settlement of my lawsuit against the railroad company.

I immediately received an anointed touch in the spiritual realm when I went to the altar to present my offering to You. And just like it happened in the supernatural, I anticipate it happening in the natural! I purchased money and financial books at the conference in preparation for my *expected* financial breakthroughs. I want to be knowledgeable about all aspects of running the ministries and businesses you will provide for me. I want to invest my seed money wisely in order to have supernatural increase to finance the end time harvest for Your Kingdom.

God is a good God, OH YES HE IS, **and a faithful God**! God is a good God, OH YES HE IS! Yes He Is! He has restored my joy and I anticipate restoration of a husband and family as well, just like in the 42nd chapter of <u>JOB</u>! Hallelujah!!

7/13/02

There was a graduation ceremony at the Potter's House for all of *God's Leading Ladies who were loosed to lead!* I wore my cap/gown (T-shirt) and I'll never be the same!

I received my cue to move forward when Jackie McCullough preached on Isaiah 61:3. This was the same Scripture that I prophesied from on February 9th at the home going service of my family.

I shared with the church that day that this verse would be the cue to my spirit that my travailing days in prayer were over and I have received beauty for my ashes! Hallelujah and Amen, Lord, for my resurrection Scripture!

7/30/02

Lord,

I've been meditating on all that has happened to me since July 11th at *"Woman Thou Art Loosed,"* in Dallas, TX and ***I am still speechless!*** I've tried as best as I can to explain to people what transpired there. They can see the physical change in me! They *"see"* the healing in my presence, by my actions, and demeanor. ***I've been loosed from the spirit of heaviness, sorrow and grief, and I AM FREE!!***

I can't thank You enough! I constantly meditate on You and Your Word for guidance on where to go from here. I came back home and began remodeling my house to reflect my acceptance of the new season I am in. I bought new bedroom furnishings, a new dinette table and changed the study into a library and office for me. I guess these changes reflect where Kevin and I really spent most of our time together - our bedroom, the dining table, and his office. I also changed the answering machine message from the old one with his voice to mine. I bought a new machine and kept the old one with his voice taped on it. I'm slowly redoing the house and pray I'll be finished by Christmas with all the details.

On July 23rd as Miriam and I were going to dinner at our family's favorite restaurant a bird ran into my driver's side window and broke the mirror. I then asked You was this a metaphor because it happened on what would have been Kevin and mine's 13th year wedding anniversary. I wondered if that was how fast Kevin and Naomi translated to the other side. I saw the bird coming towards me just like the train engineer saw them in the SUV. I thought the bird would pull up in time before impact and the engineer didn't think (per his statement) that Kevin would try to cross the tracks with the train coming. The bird hit my mirror with a thud, bounced off the car and fell down behind me somewhere. I don't know if it got run over by the other cars behind me or not. I thought that maybe that's how light Kevin's car felt to the train when it was hit and they bounced off the track after impact. The train kept going like I did and had to look back to see what had happened. Just like the train, my car sustained minimal damage, only a cracked mirror for me (I don't really know what happened to the train). That bird died on impact, so did Kevin. I don't know what happened to the second bird that was flying with the one that ran into me. I assumed it was injured like Nne was but I couldn't stop to see the results of the impact due to traffic.

I just wondered over and over if that was a visual analogy for my benefit to help me to understand how fast Kevin died. With the date being our 13th wedding anniversary, were You trying to say to me – **Kevin Is DEAD! Just like that bird died, your wedding anniversary died that quickly and is NO more! Do you get it now, Bernice?!**

I also just came back (again) from New Orleans, where I attended a funeral on yesterday. My cousin Tantreese's husband died of cancer last week. She is left, like me, to be a young widow and asked that I attend the funeral as moral support for her and her son. I invited her to come down to visit me when the "fanfare" dies down and she needs to get away from it all.

On a positive note, I won two tickets to a concert that Kevin and Naomi would have enjoyed going to – Kirk Franklin, Yolanda Adams, and Donnie McClurkin in October! I was at a Kurt Carr concert at The Fountain of Praise (Mia's church) when I won! Thanks for the FAVOR!!

I am continuing to seek Your face for details on the visions and dreams that You gave me in Dallas, TX, at WTAL'02. **I am "A Leading Lady!"** and my cue to come on stage was Kevin and Naomi's death. It turned the spotlight on me and now it's my turn. But it's all about You and not about me (like I originally thought after the accident). *It's all part of Your plan for You to get Glory from this story and for Your splendor to radiate through me to demonstrate to others Your keeping power in the midst of it all!*

"You kept me, so I wouldn't let go! God kept me!"(The verse in my heart from the same song title by Kurt Carr) You kept me in my right mind, oh yes, You did!

AUGUST

8/2/02

Isaiah 57:1-2, "The righteous pass away; the godly often die before their time. And no one seems to care or wonder why. No one seems to understand that God is protecting them from the evil to come. For the godly who die will rest in peace."

As I pondered this Scripture, I asked myself, *"**Well, what about the Godly that remain?**"*

James 1:2-4 was the prayer message that God sent to me in response to my question. God stated to me:

Bernice, whenever trouble comes your way, let it be an opportunity for JOY! For when your faith is tested, your endurance has a chance to grow. So let it grow, for when your endurance is fully developed, you will be strong in character and ready for anything!

1 Peter 1:7 was the prayer message that Kevin sent me in response to the question. Kevin stated to me:

Bern, these trials are only to test your faith, to show that it is strong and pure. It is being tested as fire tests and purifies gold – your faith is far more precious to God than mere gold. So if your faith remains strong after being tried by fiery trials; it will bring you much praise and glory on the day when Jesus Christ is revealed to the whole world.

1 Peter 4:12-13, 19; 5:10 was the prayer message that Naomi sent me in response to the question Naomi stated to me:

Momma, don't be surprised at the fiery trials you are going through, as if something strange were happening to you. Instead be very glad – because these trials will make you partners with Christ in His sufferings, and afterward you will have the wonderful joy of sharing his glory when it is displayed to the entire world. So if you are suffering according to God's will, keep on doing what is right, and trust yourself to the God who made you, for He will restore, support, and strengthen you, Momma, and He will place you on a firm foundation. My purpose in writing this message is to encourage you and assure you that the Grace of God is with you no matter what happens.

**Peace and love to you always,
God, KD, and ND**

8/3/02

"*Lord, I know I've been changed! Lord, I know I've been changed! Lord, I know I've been changed! The angels in heaven done signed my name!*" (*From the traditional spiritual version of the song found in the Baptist hymnal that is resonating in my heart*)

I felt like I had a set back this week, even though I know I was healed and delivered from my grief and sorrow in Dallas, TX, at the WTAL'02 Conference. I felt a tremendous longing for Kevin and Nne this weekend. We all (Nne, Kevin, Mmi and me) would have been planning to go back to school this weekend, now it's only Mmi and I who are going back to school this fall. *What a difference a year makes…*

I really didn't see this emotional trigger of preparing for back to school coming. It caught me by surprise and I had to shut down all activities this weekend to experience this new loss and to work through my grief with You. I allowed You to minister the Word to me through tapes from WTAL'02, personal prayer, praise, and purging. I needed to rest in Your presence and climb back into Your arms to be rocked in your bosom, *AGAIN!* I swung on the swing set at my school on Friday during lunch just to get away from people in order to think about how much my life has changed from this time last year. *It's been over six months since the accident and I'm still reeling from the after effects. Selah.*

God help me! Jesus keep me! I thought I was further along emotionally than this. **I know that I felt a supernatural touch, an anointing at WTAL'02, and I want to maintain that healing!** *Lord, help me to maintain my emotional healing!* **Keep me meditating on Your Word, Your promises, and Your love that has made me whole!** *I know what I know, and I know that You have healed me!* **Please strengthen me as I continue to walk through this healing process!! You are an Awesome Wonder to my soul!** *No one compares to You in all that You Do, NO ONE!* **Thank You!**

Mmi and I are experiencing health challenges as well, but by Your stripes, we are healed! I call those things that aren't as though they were – Hallelujah!

8/4/02

Lord,

Thank You for restoring my soul. I stopped everything this weekend to be watered by the Holy Spirit and He filled me (again). I was so busy with going back to work and getting Miriam back to school that our time together dwindled down to zilch. *I wasn't able to go very long without our fellowship.* I got spiritually "flat" almost immediately and had to "pull over" for servicing. I spent the weekend seeking Your face and as usual You are a rewarder of those who diligently seek You! Thank You for Your patience with me and Your unfailing love!

I went to Kainos Community Church today and told Pastor Joe that You had directed me to take care of getting the building painted on the outside. I heard You tell me this at their last service in their

"*My #1 Is Still My #1!*"

old building, but I thought someone else would cover that expensive cost and I would do something cheaper for them. I have visited them three times since they've moved to their new building and every time I look at the building I am reminded of what You directed me to do. So today I asked Pastor Joe how much it would cost to get the job done and told him to get estimates so that we could finish the paint job by September. Thanks for trusting me to do what You direct me to do with Your finances. I asked You to trust me to become a Distribution Center for Wealth in the Body of Christ and You are allowing me to do just that. I pray that my obedience proves to You that I can be trusted with even more finances to distribute in Your Kingdom.

I've been on both ends:

1. Receiving - when someone You directed to bless me was obedient.
2. Waiting - when someone You had directed to bless me was disobedient.

I remember how frustrated Kevin and I were while *waiting for people You directed to bless us, didn't bless us because of their disobedience.* We said that if You ever allowed us to be in the position to give, we would, so I am. Money definitely answers all!

The world system we operate in and **Your Kingdom needs Spirit filled, obedient Christians with money who will finance the end time harvest!** I signed up for that detail in Your army back when I first heard You were recruiting for the position (smile). I do remember reading in Proverbs 10:22 where You said my blessing would make me rich without sorrow, what happened? I am very sorrowful over my loss of Kevin and Naomi, what gives?

I continue to thank You for the money mentors that You are sending my way. I continue to study money topics to change, transform and renew my mind regarding money matters. Thank You for raising up people who can help me with the plans You have for me to prosper, and to carry out the vision and dreams You have given me!

You are absolutely outstanding and awesome in all Your ways!

"My #1 Is Still My #1!"

8/5/02

Lord,

*God, can I ask You (again) why did You let Kevin go over the tracks to be hit by an oncoming train? Why didn't the prayers we prayed for safety and protection cover him at that moment? Why did both he **and** Naomi have to die? Why didn't You let me go to pick up the girls to save this catastrophe from happening? I had a mind to go pick up the girls but I was constrained (by the Holy Spirit) not to call Kevin, nor go and pick up the girls. Would it have changed anything? Would Kevin have been in the accident alone or even spared?*

I miss him in the flesh! I miss You loving me through him. I know what good love feels like and I am missing it. When I was at home on bed rest during my pregnancy with Miriam at least we could cuddle, kiss and hug one another. I have no affection but that given to me by Miriam. She hugs me and loves me up a whole bunch but that's NOT the same as male and female love relations - *You know*?! This back to school season is really bumming me out! Kevin and I had a back to school weekend ritual that I can't carry out without him. I need him here to have our back to school love-a-thon. *No Kevin! No love-a-thon!!* ☹ Yuck!

I watched old videos of Nne and Kevin all day yesterday and it made me real nostalgic. I remembered the great times we had together when Nne was Mmi's age and I remember it like it was yesterday! I can't believe how much Miriam looks like Naomi at that age. It still seems like they could be twins if not for the age difference. Miriam kept looking at the tape because she didn't remember that activity and thought she was seeing herself. Most of the tapes have Kevin behind the camera with only his voice recorded. Not many pictures of him, or shots of him with Naomi.

They are together with YOU, now!! I still can't believe all I have of them is their ashes!!! Will I ever be able to part with their remains? I'm going on a cruise this September with my sisters Charlotta and Jeanette. Will I be able to spread their ashes then? Will I ever be ready to let their ashes go? God, please help me!! My spirit, my spirit, my spirit *<u>weeps for both of them</u>!!!* My spirit would REALLY need to be built up for me to be able to do that! I don't know if I'm ready to do that!! Even with me being a *"God's Leading Lady"* graduate and healed emotionally and spiritually of my grief, sorrow and heaviness over my losses that is a **REALLY HUGE** step!

I've taken off Kevin's wedding ring.
I've changed out the bedroom furniture.
I've changed out the dining room furniture.
I've changed out the office into a study.
I've taken down the posters with their pictures on it.
I've started the K&N Dickey Scholarship Fund in their memory and established it as a 501(c) 3.

CAN I TAKE A BREATHER ALREADY?

Is it You or I that is trying to move me so fast through this process?

Sometimes I can keep up with the pace, other times I want to know what the rush is. Who's running this race anyway, my FLESH or my SPIRIT? Please, let me know!!

Help me Father! Help me Jesus! Help Me Holy Ghost!! I need *tremendous* support!! Strengthen me as I go through this healing process and don't allow me to get stuck in this any longer than I have to! **I maintain that I am healed! I'm just having a *MOMENT*, and this too shall pass! I'll get through this with God to help, Amen!**

I am also physically weak and tired from dealing with Miriam and her teething, she is in pain and *everybody knows about it! She's not holding back about her teething pain for anyone! I am so sleep deprived from dealing with this girl, alone! Send me some relief!*

8/6/02

Lord, Lord, Lord!

Thanks for answering my prayers on meeting with money mentors in regards to investing options. Now I need to know if I can trust that they know what they are doing financially. I don't know if their advice will be complimentary or adversarial to Your investment style for me yet. Both of the financial planners I met with are more conservative than I am about investing for the Kingdom Harvest. I'm still prayerfully discerning if they should be on my team and/or if I am their assignment. I'm wondering if I can trust my estate planner as well because I need to discern his commitment level to You, also. I will continue praying on all of these financial relationships. If they are all sold out to You, then they won't try to take advantage of me. This strategy worked for me when I was looking for a husband 13 years ago and it should work again for me as I look for financial planners and advisors as well. *If it ain't broke, don't fix it, right?*

The details of caring for Miriam and getting her to go to sleep early are **exhausting for me!** I still can't get to bed before 10:30P.M. I need to get to bed earlier in order to get a good night's sleep for work. For me, that's eight to ten hours of sleep, **HELP!!**

Lord, be Psalms 32:8 to me, *"I will instruct you and teach you in the way you should go; I will counsel you and watch over you."*

8/8/02

Lord,

Are You pleased with my response to this tragedy? Have I modeled appropriately the correct response to this trial? I know everybody is watching me to see if and when I'll become unglued publicly because they can't believe that You are the one sustaining me.

I <u>know</u> it's been only You and none of ME! I give You all the praise and glory for this marvelous thing You've done in and through me!

I was talking to one of my prayer partners, Carolyn Clansy, on yesterday and she said that my response hasn't gone unnoticed by You. She stated that You were well pleased. Was that You speaking through her as a mouthpiece to me? I thank You for Your loving kindness that You have shown me through her words of encouragement. She has truly spoken strength into my spirit (inner man) on many occasions.

On another note, I want to thank You (again) that the passersby who saved Miriam were called by You. They were all Christian men who were submitted to Your leading to risk (not really because You were in charge) their lives to get Miriam out of the car before the explosion.

Thank You, Lord that I still have JOYFUL MMI!!

Out of all the cars that passed the accident, twelve stopped and five went in the fire! Twelve symbolizes administration, five is symbolic of grace. Hallelujah!!

8/9/02

Lord,

As I was watching Bishop T.D. Jakes tonight at his Manpower '02 Conference, I realized that we (Kevin and I) had been following him for a very long time. I remembered how Bishop's teaching and preaching transformed Kevin and I and encouraged us in the ministry. I began interceding for the men at the Manpower Conference that they will hearken to his words from the conference and be restored and made whole like I was at WTAL'02.

Who knows (but You) if my next (future) husband is not in attendance at this Manpower Conference or watching it and needs my prayer support in order to break free from his own issues? There were over 25,000 men attending the conference and many more watching by satellite in prison, some on their computers, and others by TV. My next husband may very well be in any one of those audiences and he needs his "Eve" (me) to stand in the gap for his victory. My name, *Bernice,* means bringer of victory so here we are touching and agreeing in the spirit for deliverance from and victory over every evil, in the Name of Jesus! I know not to question You or your methods any more, just do what You ask me to do because I will be the one who benefits from my obedience at Your appointed time.

I missed Kevin tremendously while watching this program. I thought of him the whole time I was watching it, knowing that he would have enjoyed this year's theme of *"Man on a Mission!"* Oh Kevin, why have you *"gone home"* ahead of me? Why didn't you wait for me? Now, I'm all alone without you and we had planned to grow old together, remember? I miss you so much — <u>*you were my very best friend in this entire world*</u> – the one I talked to about everything. Now, I only talk to Jesus, God, and the Holy Ghost and a few select friends at other times for some things. *I still love you and I have many fond memories of us (sigh).*

8/10/02

Lord, Jesus — strengthen me! I sorely miss Naomi and Kevin and August is ranking third after May (first) and April (second) as difficult months for me emotionally. My sisters are not here to help me through this month like they were for the other ones! Help! Every day, all day I am leaning on You! None of me, but all of You! **Help me, Lord!!**

This moment in time is a precursor to loose something wonderful in the spiritual realm for me, *right?* An indication of something great getting ready to happen in my life, *right?* The shaking and trembling I experienced as I laid down for a nap today scared me! The pain I felt wasn't as intense as before but was intense nonetheless. My flesh cannot handle the enormity of this loss! *Not At All! NOT-AT-ALL!!*

All of You and none of me is what have kept me since January 31, 2002! All of You and none of me! **Not at all!** Only You, God, have brought me to this date! It's in You that I have my being! You are my source, my power, and my energy! Only You can get me through this travailing, the moment before my hour of delivery! Why do I always experience deep travailing in my sleep? Is it because I'm alone and by myself? Does that allow my subconscious to let my grief come through? What is this all about? What's about to happen? What am I about to give birth to? The pain is more intense now, just like labor pains! I can't ignore or suppress it! Come on with it! Lord, let's get this on! Let's give birth to this blessing from God! Clarity of vision and the wisdom to execute it all *is my goal!*

The greater the sorrow, the greater the joy! Right? I have died (*again*) to my will, so that Christ himself may live in and through me! Am I ready now for what You have prepared for me? The object of my sorrow has become the subject of my sorrow! Can I talk about it, can I shout about it? Has my book come forth? (*In my spirit, I sense that my book about this grief experience will become an international bestseller☺ because everybody can relate to losing their loved ones.*)

When I come up out of this grave I will not remember my travailing anymore! Right?! I decree and declare that I will receive power (anointing) to mess up the 21st century - for my joy *will exceed* my sorrow! Joy *will overtake* me! My power (anointing) *will supersede* my sorrow! Hallelujah! I won't remember this pain any longer! My travail will be over! You will have exchanged all my sorrow for joy unspeakable! The kind of joy that the world can't take away! Thank You, Lord, for leading me to watch the video tape with Jackie McCullough again from the *"Woman Thou Art Loosed (WTAL), 2002"* Conference! Hallelujah for restoration, again!

I am daring to believe that my remaining days on earth will be better than my past! Even my past as Kevin's wife and Naomi's mother! Better than the wonderful marriage and family I had with them! My hope is absolutely centered in Christ Jesus! Hallelujah! I still believe *"The Best Is Yet To Come"* for me! I am confident about tomorrow because I walk with God today! He alone is the source of my strength! I trust that God does all things well as I wait on Him. Thank You, Holy Spirit and Jesus for comforting me and moving me away from my sorrow tonight! Hallelujah!

8/11/02

This date is the one month anniversary of WTAL'02 *and* my deliverance from grief and sorrow. This weekend is also the sixth month anniversary weekend of the home going services for Kevin and Naomi Dickey.

Lord, while I was sleeping my *"spirit man"* travailed for me in **deep sorrow**. It was so intense that it woke me up and lingered on as pain. I know I need to deal with this, but how?! I don't want to ignore it, or suppress it, nor run from it, **_but LORD!_** You know all about this…how can I endure this pain? I moaned my way to church today and the groanings turned to utterances that could not wait for altar call, nor the invitation to Christ. My spirit (Holy Spirit working on the inside) was leaping out of me, directing me to join Kainos Community Church and become a new member.

When I joined, I just broke down in tears of praise and worship. I could not contain my joy or sorrow any longer. They couldn't move on in the service until they could *"reach"* me to introduce me to the church. At that same time, I felt a release in the spiritual realm like a yoke or something broke off of me! I was free! I have no idea what happened for me in the heavenlies. I just know that nobody can do me like Jesus! **Nobody!** I felt so relieved after my decision to join this church. *I must have moaned and groaned my way all the way into the Kainos Community Fellowship because my travailing was absolutely exhausting for me!*

8/12/02

Lord,
I realized that yesterday was one month to the date after I received my deliverance in Dallas, Texas at WTAL'02. I realized over the weekend that I have been delivered to the stage of "acceptance" in this grief work. It took me almost six months to accept that Kevin and Naomi are **_really dead_**. They died on January 31, 2002 and will never return home to me on this side of heaven. They are gone and now I am left all alone to cope with the meaning of the loss of their companionship.

This is why my spirit is *just now* travailing with sorrow, weeping, groaning and moaning finally allowing me to experience their loss and *my life without them*. Every day I move forward is a day farther away from January 31, 2002. I am a delayed griever and I have had a hard time getting in touch with my emotions and grief about this loss. Every time I feel like its coming up my throat from the pit of my stomach I swallow it down again.

"My #1 Is Still My #1!"

The emotional pain still causes me to shake, quake and tremble in my body when I feel it. I can't bear this emotional pain manifesting in my flesh! Staying in the Spirit is the only way that I can go on, keep on keeping on, and pressing on! To allow all of my sorrow to come up out of me will drown me, *won't it?* How will I be able to function and be mentally present for Miriam if I allow all of this pain to come up? When will I have time to fully experience my emotional reaction to this? All of my negative feelings, grief, and sorrow scare me because I am not comfortable with experiencing such strong emotions.

Lord, how do I give in to this? Will I be able to function when I let these emotions take over? Lord, can't You just turn my sorrow into joy! Do I really need to experience the depth of my sorrow in order to exchange it for joy? I do know this much that I have absolutely and totally disconnected from my feelings throughout this experience. I have completely shut down emotionally because of this trauma. Emotionally, I can't relate nor do I want to relate to it. What do I do next? Direct me, and guide me in the way I should go. Lord, I'm hurting deeply! I'm hurting real deep down inside my being, down to my core, and my spirit, my inner man. ***Help me!!***

8/17/02

Lord,

I have had a full feast and great fellowship with You since Wednesday night of last week. I watched Juanita Bynum on television on Wednesday and Thursday. I went to the Women's Fellowship "*Joy for the Journey*" on Friday night at my new church (Kainos Community). I also attended a Women's Conference all day today. I feel stacked up in the Word of God like I couldn't eat one more morsel of it. *I am so full - where would anymore of it go?*

As I was leaving a birthday party that Miriam and I had attended, I decided to swing by my mother-in-law Laverne's house since I was in the area. I was talking with her on my cell phone while driving and I came upon an automobile train collision one intersection down from where Kevin and Naomi died! I couldn't believe what I saw!

There I was driving on Highway 90, just past the intersection where Kevin and Naomi died and I stumbled upon another auto and train wreck! What the hell is going on here?

That vehicle was a car, smaller than our SUV. The front of it was intact but the rear was torn off and dragged down the tracks. An ambulance was on the Highway 90 side of the railroad track to put the accident victim inside of it, while the fire truck was on the other side of the railroad tracks. I looked at that scene and saw instead *my own family's traffic accident scene moving in slow motion* along with all the witnesses to it! There were two cars parked on the side of the road and auto-parts dragged alongside the railroad tracks. The conductor was inside the train leaning against the window of his boxcar about 100 feet away from the point of impact.

The ambulance then proceeded to come up behind me to go through traffic to get the accident victim to the hospital. I was paralyzed and traumatized to come upon the scene, then stunned to see the ambulance come up *behind me*, of all people? I could hardly pull over to the side of the road for the ambulance to pass. I parked my car and cried my eyes out. I hung up the phone with Laverne and tried to get myself together after witnessing such déjà-vu events. I eventually calmed down enough to get myself together to drive on over to my mother-in-law's house. I couldn't believe what I had just experienced and sat down on her couch calling out Your Name, *Jesus, Jesus, Jesus!* What on earth is going on? *Why did You allow me to witness that accident scene?* Lord, what in the world was that about??? And the timing was too strategic NOT TO BE a set up from Satan! This was too much for me and I couldn't stop shaking my head over these events and wondering what was that really all about?

8/18/02

After church today and after talking with my sisters, I realized something. I must be on the verge of another breakthrough emotionally, spiritually, and financially! The collective revisits to tragic situations by all three of us sisters this weekend is because of a shared upcoming breakthrough for us! My revisit was the traffic accident

"My #1 Is Still My #1!"

on yesterday and Charlotta and Jeanette had a hospital revisit with Earl's (Jeanette ex-husband's) mom. She had a stroke yesterday and is in a deep coma. The tragic revisit at the hospital was that the doctor who is working on Earl's mom is the same doctor that worked on our mom 11 years ago in September before she died. He remembered my sisters from that experience and asked them how they were doing. So in a span of 24 hours we, *The Bright Sisters*, have revisited two emotionally traumatic events for us.

All I could surmise about my revisit is this: it was Naomi and Kevin's destiny to die on January 31, 2002 *at that time*. Just this week, two more people were hit by oncoming trains, the same train company that hit Kevin and Naomi, and **they survived!** One truck was hit and got turned over. The driver was only ticketed! In the other accident (*The one I witnessed*) the driver was brought by ambulance to the hospital and is doing fine! The only damage done was that the rear of his car was torn off and dragged down the railroad tracks! The fact of the matter here is that they both survived, **which is my point exactly!** We hear all the time on the news about people getting hit and surviving a train accident - **even Miriam survived our train wreck!** The difference for Kevin and Naomi was that our car exploded on impact and burned them beyond recognition after the accident! This brings me back to my final conclusion that *it was their time to "go home" to be with their Lord!*

It's really good to know that they have each other and are away from here. They don't have to go through this world's trials and tribulations anymore. Here we are Jeanette, Charlotta, Earl's family, and I dealing with the possible home going of Earl's mom to join Kevin and Naomi in heaven this year! She was here in Houston for me just over six months ago, now she is *"going home to be with the Lord"* in the same year!

I am glad that they get to "go home!" They all had a personal relationship with You so I celebrate that they are home with You in heaven. Their leaving is bittersweet. Bitter for us left behind, sweet for them because they are at rest! Yippee for them! **Ugh** for us! We remain yet another day to labor on this side of heaven. One day, shortly, we will all join them in heaven and they will say to us, *"we have been waiting for you all!"*

"My #1 Is Still My #1!"

I think it's absolutely remarkable that I rebounded as quickly as I did from witnessing a train accident on yesterday. I guess You showed me that I am stronger than I thought and further along emotionally than I knew. You are Awesome! I went back and forth from praising You to still being in awe of You! I can't believe how You are answering my prayers for a speedy recovery and healing from this revisit of grief! Restoration, restitution, and recompense all form a three-fold cord for me! Hallelujah!

Jeanette said that maybe the car that was hit by the train on yesterday was stalled on the tracks because a "live" train on the tracks drains the battery and the engine may have stopped on the person driving. That might have been what happened with Kevin and Naomi also, but our tragedy was that the car exploded after impact. I know that both Naomi and Miriam survived the impact and that the fire from the explosion consumed Naomi! So my story ended differently than the other two this week - it wasn't those people's time to die - *but it was Kevin and Naomi's.*

Romans 8:26 - I realized over the weekend that the deep travail that I had been experiencing is similar to the travail I felt at the time of the accident. I was in the bed trying to sleep around the time of the accident. I fell off to sleep around 5:20 P.M. I woke up with knots in my stomach over the next 20 minutes, not able to utter a word, as if I was constrained or muzzled. I now realize that it was the Holy Spirit in me knowing what I was about to go through and He was beginning the intercession for me as I laid down awaiting their arrival. Romans 8:27 - It was this same Holy Spirit that finally allowed me to get up from bed around 5:45P.M. and I looked at the clock and decided to get dinner on the table. It was the voice of the Holy Spirit that urged me to eat right at 6 P.M. because we were on a church fast that brought us together as a family at 6 P.M. for dinner, over the past 17 days. He got me to eat because I would need my strength for "later."

I did eat and decided to watch the news while I ate. I saw the lead in story about an accident and began praying for the family of the middle aged man and his teenage daughter. I continued to eat and tried to reach Kevin by cell phone to tell him about *the accident but it only rang and rang. I finished eating and was perplexed by the oddity that Kevin would not answer his phone and the answering service wasn't coming on either. I saw an update on the news report and heard that they had rescued an infant girl before the car exploded. I realized that they had called my Kevin the middle aged man and my Nne a teenager when I saw my car on fire by the railroad tracks on Cravens Road! That was the route we usually took home after we picked up the girls from school! The headline news was mine! Half of my family had just perished! My world had just changed! My testing of faith had begun!*

Again Lord, I pray that I have represented You well as I go through this testing of my faith! That I have demonstrated what trust and faith in You could do for a believer! Amen! There is only one person's approval that I am seeking! Only one person's opinion that I care to be favorable and *that's You GOD! My World! My Confidant! My Friend! My Guide! My Comforter! My true Deliverer!* **Daily do I seek Your face! Diligently do I seek Your face and I definitely want Your will for my life, even if it's without Kevin and Naomi.**

I know that You know what's best for me and I accept how You are running things in my life. I trust that You are working it out for my good according to Your purpose, <u>Romans 8:28</u>. Hallelujah!

8/19/02

Thank You Lord for restoring my soul! I was exhausted and spent emotionally after receiving the news that Earl's Mom had died this morning. I wanted to be there for my sisters and here I was alone in Houston understanding what they were going through in New Orleans. I needed strength for the day and You gave it to me!

Thank You for a great place for me to work at while I've been going through this trial. The whole staff has been excellent and understanding of me when I have been triggered emotionally by memories and/or present events.

I read Wanda Turner's book, *"Celebrating Change,"* where she talked about throwing herself a party to celebrate her season of widowhood in an attempt to embrace it and I ran with the idea for myself. The details of my own *"Celebrating Change"* Praise Party are coming along fine. The people I chose to invite are all available on September 21, 2002 and we will all be pampered with services at a local Salon and Spa. I can't wait for my coming out party with my girlfriends!

8/25/02

I just got back from ministering in New Orleans to my family and Earl's family for his mom's funeral. Thank You for Your grace and mercy to make the trip. Thanks for keeping all of us, even while separated, and uniting us together again as a family!

I prayed for more details of my destiny while in New Orleans and was constantly being brought back to sermons on Joseph and Job to study as well as the book of James. ***The three J's can't beat Jesus Christ!*** As I pray and meditate on my journey through grief, I gain spiritual insight daily. I pray for direction, guidance, and wisdom to handle the responsibilities You are giving to me. *"Instruct me and teach me in the way I should go; counsel me and watch over me."* (Psalm 32:8)

I want to spend more time with You this week. Clear my schedule for us to hang out and fellowship, and keep Miriam on her schedule too! Thank You!

8/26/02

Lord,

You answered me quickly and met me at our usual meeting place, *"our prayer closet."* Father, thank You for divine purpose and the holy calling You have given me. Today I am reminded that it was You who sent me to minister and not other men or women. What You have said about me will come to pass as surely as the sun rises each day, and no one can add to or subtract from what Your decree is. Thank You in Jesus' Name that everything You have said about me is coming to pass! ***I will accomplish great exploits!!*** Help me to bring to pass the dream You put inside of me. Grant me grace to walk in obedience and faith as You stretch me and mold me. Help me to carry Your seed until it is fully revealed to the world. You are faithful in all things, and I trust You. You will keep every promise and honor every word You have spoken to me and over me, because You are faithful. Help me to be faithful too. I love You, and by Your grace I wait for the fulfillment of Your promises. Show me who will receive the dream and I will make it plain to them.

And Jesus, in advance, I thank You for the capital I will need! God, I am stirring up the gift. I remembered the dream You gave me. Please show me the partners I need to encourage me on this journey. Let it be to me according to Your Word. Lord Jesus, thank You for all the previews. Thank You for the vision of what will one day be, and thank You for allowing me to bring it to pass on earth as it is in heaven. I am pregnant with abundance and it's kicking on the inside of me! As a dreamer, I walk as a person heavy with prosperity and abundance. I must remain persistent until the supernatural happens! The trials I have gone through are all a part of the preparation process to transform my dreams and visions into realities. Hallelujah!

Thank You for creative ideas so that I can start my own businesses and prosper where others have failed. I don't need earth's money; all I need is heaven's idea. If the idea came from You God, then You will finance it. My trials and tribulations do not mess me up or rob me of my blessings, they help develop my character and that is where my true wealth lies. Thank You for the vision of what will one day come to pass. Thank You for the clues (i.e. recent deaths in my family, the vexing of my soul by friends and family to try and distract me from my vision/dream/destiny) that let me know that I am getting closer to bringing it to pass on earth as it is in heaven.

Thank You for strengthening me to press through to the end! Even though unexpected situations such as Kevin and Naomi's deaths happened they were not "unexpected" to You God. I know that something inside is telling me that something bigger, better, and greater is waiting for me, just on the other side of the middle if I just keep pressing forward until I make it to my dream. And thanks for encouraging me in this "in between" time, the things You said *will come to pass concerning me!* The devil did not win, no matter what he threw at me. Lord, I know You did not mention the "in between" part of this calling to me, because You knew I would have avoided it. I am in the middle of the middle right now, and I put all my trust in You. Only You know the beginning from the end and my future is bright and grounded in Your faithfulness. Thank You for walking through this fiery trial with me. I still remember the vision; forgive me for grumbling in this "in between" time.

Lord, I know that You are a rewarder of those who diligently seek You. With Your help, God, I decide today to diligently follow You and Your Kingdom principles. I want to do great things for You right now, and I choose to submit to Your timetable. We see time, but You work things out in their proper season. Lord Jesus, *I will not get stuck, I refuse to give up.* I want You more and more. I believe that with Your help to strengthen me, this experience will add to my destiny. I admit to feeling impatient at times. But thank You Jesus for doing all things well in my life. I trust You to move me where I must go in the fullness of time and to supply me with everything I need for success in the task You have given me, Lord.

I receive Your loving correction in the area of tithes and offerings (the particular and specific churches and ministries you designated) and I repent of every sin against You. I want to accomplish Your Kingdom's purpose in my life. I release every stubborn area of disobedience to which I cling. Lord, I hear You telling me to go forward. I sense Your courage rising up in me and I am ready to cross the river from the known to the unknown realm of faith. This is my season, and by Your Spirit, I will bear much fruit today and in the days to come! Hallelujah! In Jesus' Name, Amen!

8/30/02

All this week Mmi called me "Daddy!!" She was so excited and joyful when she called me Daddy that I answered to that name. She still calls me Momma, but when I went to pick her up from school she called me "Daddy." She has also been doing a gesture that her Dad used to do with her when we sat at the table to eat dinner. The pictures taken of her recently show her doing that gesture – she points at you as if saying, *"Right back at you."*

I ask You, is this Kevin ministering to me through Mmi? Only I would know what that gesture means and Mmi is too young to know what she is doing or who she is reminding me of when she does it. I take it as God ministering to me through Miriam and reminding me that both Naomi and Kevin's spirits are alive in her as she ministers to me with actions that remind me of them. Thank You for leaving sweet Miriam to comfort me! Thank You! Thank You! Thank You!

I am excited to be able to dispense the scholarship You have allowed me to finance through the K & N Dickey Ministries, Inc!! I received only one application by the deadline and it was an awesome one! I thank You for using me to answer this family's prayers. This *definitely* helps my emotional healing!! Thank You, Lord!

Through this scholarship fund, I can be a blessing in Your honor to another Christian family and support a child who reminds me of Nne. A child who also has strong spiritual parents like Kevin and I were for Nne. Thank You for allowing me to answer a prayer that Kevin and I prayed for ourselves during all the years that Nne went to a private Christian school. We wanted someone to do for us what You are allowing me to do for someone else now - to help a committed to You Christian middle class family keep their child in a Christian elementary school environment!

Thank You for using me as a Wealth Distribution Center!

Hallelujah!!

SEPTEMBER

9/1/02

Well, Lord, I completed the assignment You gave me to go to an exclusive shop and purchase something for myself. I bought three suits from the St. John's collection. I also bought three pairs of Van Eli shoes and matching purses on my *"dream shopping spree."* I am still waiting for You to tell me when to wear the outfits. Spending some of the money on myself instead of seeding into ministries, paying off bills, and helping out others is very uncomfortable for me. I have to get comfortable in spending money on me. I FEEL GUILTY for surviving Kevin and Naomi's accident and *I wasn't even in the car*. Because of their deaths, I have the resources to have a "dream shopping spree" without them. We always dreamed of going to a store and being able to buy whatever we wanted and money not being an object and it felt great to be able to do that! I just miss that Kevin and Naomi were not here to share the moment we always dreamed of sharing together as a family.

Jeanette was in town this weekend and shared the *"dream shopping spree"* with me by helping me to pick out which suits to buy. She even helped me pick out home furnishings to buy and gave me advice on redecorating. I bought document frames for all of the diplomas that will go up on the *"Wall of Achievement"* I am creating for the study/prayer room. This dedication to our family's academic achievements should be finished by the end of the week.

Jeanette and I are getting back to how we used to relate before she grew up and got "out there." I'm getting my "old" sister back as she seeks to walk with God and make herself available to You to be used in Your service. She's considering moving down here, I told her to fast and pray that the Lord would give her peace as she makes her decision. I told her she was welcome to stay with me if she comes down and she can possibly find a good paying job in her field – property management.

Kainos Community Church's worship service was awesome today, I magnified You the whole service and felt emotionally relieved when I departed! Thank You!

9/3/02

Lord, God – Jehovah! *Help me and my unbelief!*
Already I am thinking that I should return the items from the dream shopping spree and buy cheaper clothing or other things with my money. Am I questioning my worth? Help me to settle into this new level that You have ushered me into! I know this transition I am going through is not for naught!! I believe and feel that this is the beginning of my latter days being better than my former. I truly believe this and long to receive it! Help me to be comfortable with wealth, Holy Ghost! Help me, Lord, by fortifying my confidence!!

I have decided that the first time I will wear one of the St. John suits is when You allow me to preach the Gospel or share this incredible testimony before men and women.

Lord, I am in the process of planning my *"Celebrating Change Praise Party"* for later on this month. Please dispel the depression and nostalgia that I am experiencing over the two year anniversary of moving into our house this weekend without my Kevin and Naomi being here to share it with me.

9/4/02

Lord,
I don't remember if I had written down the details of the Prayer Vigil we held at the old church on February 1st, the day after the accident, but I want to write it out now.

As we were comforting ourselves at the church on that night, the choir was singing melodiously and the ceiling opened up in the supernatural and a searing touch came through me from the top of my head through my body and raised me to my feet. It was like a rod of steel went through me. I was picked up like a piece of meat on a fork and placed from here to there. In the spirit I saw a sword planted in the ground on the floor before me and I took it in both of my hands to lift it up out of the floor. I looked up to see where it fell from and only saw a hole in the ceiling and clouds above that. I looked around me and realized that no one else had seen what I saw, nor experienced what I had and began worshipping You. I stretched my hands and arms out to You and couldn't believe what had happened! Lord, God, Your mantle was thrown down to me from heaven at the church that night!

I know I have been released from my former church but why are my heartstrings being pulled to the old church? I still have ties to all of my other former churches, is this tie the same or more? I've been away for a long time from all of my former churches and when I visit them I still feel at home. I don't feel like returning to the old church just yet. Their rejection of me still stings even though I have realized that it was necessary for You to move me into place for my next level. Why can't I just let go and forgive them?

Help me, Lord! I know in my head that You orchestrated it all and I trust You to know what You are doing. Help me to forgive them for their part in Your plans for me. My heart needs to catch up with my head knowledge. The gap is narrowing but *there still is* a gap there for me. All of this has transpired because *"The Best Is Yet To Come for Me!"* I believe it! I'm just trying to receive it in my spirit!! I press on daily! Each day I wake up is another day towards my destiny in Christ Jesus. Please, Holy Spirit, continue to guide me in the way that I should go.

9/6/02

Lord,

    Thank You for comforting me again in my struggle to parent Mmi by myself. Single parenting is hard, tiring and exhausting with few breaks (except for the ones I choose to create for myself). I had a rough week with Mmi coming and going, long work days, with short nights and I'm pooped! From reading a book by Tony Evans on single parenting, I am comforted by the knowledge that You know my circumstances and how I got here, so You got it. Please, Lord, just continue to strengthen me as I go through this grief process in Jesus' Name. Amen.

9/7/02

Lord,

    Thank You again for reminding me that You know my circumstances. You created them and You haven't forgotten about me. I was **STRESSED OUT** this week with all of my responsibilities: work, Mmi, car trouble, meetings at work, late meetings, etc. and I was feeling under the weather as well. All of this contributed to me feeling low and possibly depressed which led to my spiraling emotionally as well. I talked to my "soul" and the "Holy Spirit" took control over me and my body this week to carry me through this entire week. Thank You, for teaching me how to press on when I am weak, for that is when You are strong and mighty, Hallelujah!

9/9/02

Lord, God, Jehovah!! Thank You for keeping me in my right mind! This morning I had a trying time – *a temptation if you would* **– to go across the railroad tracks near my job that had the railroad arms down and the lights flashing but with no train in sight!!**

    As I was praying and praising You for being Jehovah-God while driving in my car, a major distraction in the form of this temptation came to me and shook me up. I was thanking You for being my Protector, for keeping a watch over me and Miriam and for the awesome time we had together on yesterday at church. I was still praising You for the breakthrough when out of nowhere comes a guy coaxing people to go around the arms of the railroad track because no train was in sight. I saw one car go around – he made it. The guy came to my car and encouraged me to do the same. I thought about it, and then decided to call the school because I was going to stay put until the train (where ever it was on the tracks) had passed. While I was calling them, cars behind me went around me to drive around the arms that were down and across the tracks and they didn't get hit. Cars opposite the track went around the arms and crossed the tracks and they didn't get hit. I started sobbing hard as I spoke to Triny, our school secretary, because I couldn't move (nor did I want to) to go around the arms to go across the tracks like the others did because **"I WOULD BE THE ONE TO GET HIT BY THE TRAIN!"** I cried to her over the phone. She said for me to stay right there in line and she would send someone over to come and get me. I was suffering a panic attack and became paralyzed.

Finally, I was able to move my car into the parking lot next to where I was in line and let it all go to cry, uncontrollably. I wondered if that was what had happened to Kevin and Naomi. I immediately wanted to go home and crawl into bed with the covers pulled over me. I couldn't compose myself to drive home. I told myself, "NO" that's what the devil wants me to do. I'll stay put until my help comes. I stayed and cried as I watched how people crossed the tracks around the railroad arms, even my district's school bus with children on it went around the railroad arms!! I shook my head in disbelief as I watched this and continued to cry. I leaned over on the car seat to prevent my seeing anymore railroad crossings. In the case of an accident occurring, I didn't want to witness it. Plus, I was too paralyzed by my panic attack to drive anywhere else. I stayed put until my two angels, Minnie and Mary from the front office, came to drive me and my car over to the school.

As we drove back to school, we found out that the other intersections on either side of the intersection where I was – *was clear, with no arms down, and no lights flashing!* But, as we looked down from where we crossed over the tracks, we did see a train on the tracks! And as we parked at the school and entered the building, we heard the train's whistle blow as it was passing where we had just left it on the tracks. It wasn't until I talked it over with Mary, our school counselor, that we realized that this was a trick of the enemy to scare me to "retreat back" away from the destiny You have planned for me. I wanted to go home and stay in bed – *forever* – after that scare and magnification of what could have happened to Kevin and Naomi. It really shook me up, but I refused to be bullied by this customized temptation from the devil to get me to retreat and back-up off of my destiny! **HELL-TO-THE-NO! *Not after everything I've already lost, the devil is a liar!***

FIERCE CONFIDENCE *is what is building up in me now! The devil is defeated because I have the victory in Jesus' Name! Thank You for keeping me until my help came. Thank You (again) for the staff at my school who were compassionate and understanding of the emotional triggers I suffer from regularly on this journey through grief. Hallelujah!! I won again!*

9/12/02

Lord,

I am growing real excited about my *"Celebrating Change Praise Party"* on 9/21/02 at the spa. My guest list is confirmed and now I'm planning the details for the souvenirs. Anticipation is rising among my guests as well. They don't know who else is coming besides themselves and it will be a surprise to them all. This is a dream come true party for me to be able to pamper those who have poured spiritual life back into me. What a wonderful way for me to show them my appreciation for what they have done so far in my journey through grief. Each lady is special to me and seven have confirmed. Eight is the number of new beginnings and seven is the number of completion. Including me, eight people will attend my **"CELEBRATING CHANGE** *Praise Party"* next Saturday. To God, be the Glory, for this marvelous thing He has done in giving me the idea for this party!

I had a *very challenging week,* all this week, but You kept me through it all and I bless and praise You for this week's blessings. After an awesome Sunday of tremendous Praise and Worship, I was prepared for the challenges that came day after day this week. Thank You for preparing me and for keeping me in my right mind, which I so desperately needed, Hallelujah!

9/13/02

You, God, test me and sustain me at the same time! I realized a few months ago that it's not about me, but it's all about You and *for You* to get the glory from Your strength manifested in me! You are an Awesome Wonder! No one compares to You!

This experience has so-o-o emptied me of *"me!"* I am broken in places that I'm still finding out about as I journey through this process. When I think of being shattered, I think of finding pieces of the broken item even months later as one goes about cleaning up a room. You find tiny pieces embedded in things you hadn't seen the first time, second time, or even the third time that you "swept" the room. I'm still removing "broken pieces" from my body, heart, and soul that were penetrated by this trial. Some of Kevin's family members went out and got physical tattoos in memory of my family. I carry the emotional tattoos of them which remain in me as a testament of their impact on my life everyday.

As I pray, purge, and repent, more sorrow comes up to the surface and I continue to find something else in myself to work on. I want to get to the place where remembering won't cause my tender soul to sting when I reflect on this test of my faith. I'm still healing, and in some places I'm picking shatterings out of my blood soaked soul, and I hurt, not like before when I felt like I was hemorrhaging, but I ache just the same. I look back over my journey this year so far and I know how far You've brought me – Hallelujah! It's You, who has kept me and blessed me beyond measure! Thanks for ministering to me through willing vessels here on earth. *Thank You for being **MY SOURCE!!!*** I trust You and pray that I have proven that I can be trusted by You!! This is a very hard concept that I had to grasp regarding this fiery, testing, trial of my faith.

"My #1 Is Still My #1!"

9/15/02

Lord,

Your Holy Spirit's anointing has been upon me this whole weekend. Keeping me, acknowledging me, correcting my faulty thinking, and keeping me on the path You have ordained for me.

Today was an awesome day in the Spirit for me even though I was severely tempted to go back and visit my old church today. You ministered strongly to me in church service *and* in Sunday school class. You showed me why I have been tempted all week long on last night at the WTAL'02 Reunion Party. The ladies I went to the WTAL'02 Conference with have formed an accountability group for us as a follow up to check in with each other on the visions we were going to walk in after the conference.

You showed me at that WTAL'02 Reunion Party that others can still see Your anointing on my life in spite of the trial I am coming through. Last night I was asked by the host to minister to all the *"Leading Ladies"* from the WTAL'02 Conference through prayer and personal testimony. Today I was asked by the teacher of my Sunday school class to take over her spot as a co-teacher because she thought I could handle it. We are studying the book of James and as You know, I have been living out the book of James on spiritual maturity in Christ since 1/31/02 of this year. So it was easy for me to say, "No problem!"

You do remember, Lord, that I stood on the Scriptures from James 1:2-4 for strength at the funeral of Kevin and Naomi, right? You, Lord, *only You*, have allowed for my gift of teaching to make room for me at this church because of our lively class discussions! You alone are my Redeemer, my Restorer, and my Recompenser. *I trust You for my total restoration and **DOUBLE** for my trouble, Hallelujah!*

9/17/02

Lord,

I was watching a TV program and they were showing a father/daughter dance and I realized that Kevin would have really enjoyed attending a dance with Miriam and how much she was going to miss out on with never getting to know her real Dad. He died when she was so young (13 months) and she won't ever get to meet him. He wouldn't have missed out on anything like this with her and now he's missing out on her whole life.

I couldn't hold back the tears from falling and I began bawling, crying, hollering, and screaming! Miriam joined in! She didn't know why she was crying only that I was crying and she shared my grief with me, she screamed, she hollered and she went off into a corner all by herself and I had to go after her to comfort her. I got tissues for our eyes and she wiped her eyes and mine. It was so sweet! My heart was aching, absolutely twisted through the wringer and here was Miriam ministering to me as I cried and smiled!

Thank You for wiping the tears from my eyes through Miriam. Thank You for being there through Miriam, praying through Miriam for me when she said, *"Jesus, help you Momma."* She raised her hands to imitate me as I lifted mine up when I shouted, **"Jesus, help me!"** She said, *"Jesus help you"* and pointed to me! What wonderful intercession that Miriam prayed for her Mommy☺!

9/18/02

Lord, God!!!

You are awesome in this place (my house) Almighty God!! I received Your response to my verbal (not written) prayer petition from 8/29/02, twenty one days ago on today! Initially, Kevin's former employer had decided that they would not pay me for Kevin's personal leave time left in his account (its equivalent to vacation time). Today I received a call from them informing me that they reversed their decision and would cut and mail me a check for half of his time owed to me shortly! Hallelujah!! I stood on Your Word and refused to accept their word as final. I believed Your report that You are my source! Hallelujah!! You proved Yourself again! Amen and Hallelujah!!

"My #1 Is Still My #1!"

9/22/02

Today I am rejoicing because not only did I receive a check from Kevin's former employer, I received payment for the entire amount of leave time that was due to me! They had originally promised to only give me half of his personal leave time, then for some reason ***(I know it was YOU)*** they went ahead and paid me for all of it! Hallelujah! What an awesome God I serve! Thank You for looking out for this young widow and her orphan! You did it again!

I was feeling scared and melancholy because I am pressing on toward the mark of the higher calling in Christ Jesus and that means moving into position to be blessed at Kainos Community Church and breaking the soul ties with my old church. I feel like I am often tempted to look back like Lot's wife at what I'm leaving and not watching what's ahead. I pray earnestly for the strength to remain focused and steadfast as You sustain me while I stay on my path to healing. I know that He who began a good work in me is faithful to complete it in me! You aren't finished with me yet! I can't wait for the next level!

Thank You for allowing me to have the Praise Party on yesterday! It was totally awesome and anointed! Your presence permeated the atmosphere of the whole spa! The other clients "sensed something" (the supernatural) was going on in our private room because we had a great time in YOU!! You allowed me to share with each special lady how You used her to minister to me. I thanked them for their obedience to You and how their obedience <u>absolutely kept me</u> from spiraling downward. You directed each one of them to walk alongside me just when I needed to be encouraged the most and You met my needs through them and I just wanted to show them my appreciation. I shared with them what You have revealed to me in the way of ministry and business enterprises. You, God, were praised for Your Sovereignty and faithfulness by us all!!

OCTOBER

~~∻~~

10/4/02

Defining moment as referenced in Joshua 1:1

"*Now after*" **the death of Kevin, my husband, and Naomi, my daughter, I reckon my past life as a wife and mother of two as DEAD! I'm going on without them, my past is DEAD! Even though my life with them was strong up until the end, God said that my former life, I will see no more! It's time for my new experience beyond my pain that's worth living for! God wouldn't allow me to survive and not allow me to succeed! If I had needed Kevin and Naomi for this future, God would have let them live. But they are gone – DEAD! Forgetting those things that are behind and reaching forward to those things ahead, I press toward …***my new beginning!***

I just got back from the cruise with my sisters, Charlotta and Jeanette. I laughed again! I had fun again! I had a great time for the first time since the accident! I didn't think that I could laugh like that again, or enjoy myself again and it was absolutely therapeutic and medicinal! I felt like I laughed myself back to healthy LIFE! I giggled most of the trip with my sisters and it was definitely beneficial for my soul!! We fussed, but laughed more, just as sisters do!!

I felt liberated from myself. Free to be **"*Bern*,"** not Sister Dickey, not Mrs. Dickey, not Miriam's Mom, Kevin's widow, nor Naomi's Mom –**"*Just Bern*"** and it unlocked something in me – I felt a *"pop"* in the Holy Spirit! **I don't know if the old *"Bern"* came up or the *"new survivor Bern"* was birthed.** Only God knows! I pray that the new survivor Bern is what popped up and out! I've gone through too much to go back, I need to keep it moving forward. I've been feeding my spirit in order to keep on fighting, to press in, and to hear clearly from You, God!

I heard Your voice say clearly on the cruise that it was time to spread Kevin and Naomi's ashes, and I did so, promptly! I had brought their ashes with me just in case I was strong enough to cast their remains upon the waters. You strengthened me, as well as my sisters, as I obeyed You. But, immediately afterwards, a spirit of suicide came over me so strongly that I wanted to jump in the water after the ashes. I struggled with the thought until I finally overcame it by thinking of my sisters and Miriam and what they would have to go through on top of everything else. I was able to verbally cast down the thought of jumping overboard in the Name of Jesus and quickly ran inside the ship to get away. My spirit *and* flesh cooperated together to carry me away from the ledge. Hallelujah!

After I completed the assignment of spreading my family's ashes, my sisters were able to comfort me with **YOUR** *strength.* Jeanette's Pastor and wife were onboard the cruise and they prayed for all three of us when we went to their state room for comfort. **I REALLY NEEDED PRAYER!** *I needed Your reassurance that I would be able to go on with my life without Kevin and Naomi.* The act of casting their ashes on the sea resonated in my soul. I was at a stage in my grief journey that I didn't recognize that I was at. *I was astonished by how much God had strengthened me to do the assignment He asked me to do! WOW!*

God, You have chosen me for such a time as this!! You are moving me through this at a rate swifter than others because I am chosen and have been given supernatural favor from You! You've snatched me from so many things, Hallelujah! Thank You, Lord, for I am chosen! Even when I was knocked down from the "double gut punch" of multiple losses on 1/31/02, I was still chosen by You – to survive all of my trials and temptations before I was even formed in my mother's womb. As I walk in this spiri-

tual knowledge of being chosen by You, God, I have peace!! My help cometh from You, Lord, from You ALONE! You chose me and ordained me!! You have ordered my steps! My steps have been ordered by the Lord! Not one weapon formed against me, shall prosper! Hallelujah!

I am chosen...
    ...to be BLESSED!
    ...to be an overcomer!
    ...to be spoiled by You!
    ...to have the favor of God!
I am ordained...
    ...to be fruitful!!
    ...to have my fruit to REMAIN!!

God will sustain my success!!!
God will maintain my prosperity!!!
God will teach me to walk in the integrity of what He has spoken over me!!!
Hallelujah!!!

Not one word that You have spoken over me shall return unto You VOID!!!
But it shall accomplish what You purposed!!!
Hallelujah!! Amen!! Thank You, Jesus!!!

10/7/02

Miriam made (22) months today!

    You blessed me today to have my car go out near my mother-in-law's house. My brother-in-law was able to come to my rescue and get my car back up and running again. Amen and Hallelujah! Kevin and Naomi died in the newer car and I still have this older car to deal with. If I had had a choice in the matter, I would have chosen for them to die in this car instead of the newer one, you know? Oh, well...

"My #1 Is Still My #1!"

Thank You for ordering my steps to my additional job assignment today. The students and staff at my new school were welcoming, but now I am the Assistant Principal at **two** elementary schools! ***Lord, give me strength!***

My only challenge today was in trying to discern why people at my former church were pursuing me in calls and leaving messages saying they were thinking of me. I sent word to them that Miriam and I were doing fine and to keep praying for our strength. I'm still working through my anger at those church folk. I need more space to resolve things and to step back from my bad experiences with them at the old church.

I'm still hurt by their actions and spiritual immaturity and my emotional wound is still tender, though healing. It needs to be tended to by the consistent application of the Word of God to the areas of anger, bitterness, and unforgiviness before reconciliation can take place. I pray for healing in these areas and know just as You have come through before in other areas of healing for me that You are faithful to fulfill this request as well. I want total and complete healing and a proper understanding of forgiveness. What does real forgiveness look like in the Scriptures? I know You to be a rewarder of those who diligently seek You, so I'm anticipating Your reward to me as I seek You on this one.

I packed up Nne and Kevin's belongings and will place them in Laverne's care for the time being. They needed to be put away, which was my immediate assignment from You when I returned from the cruise with my sisters. I procrastinated, but I finally did it when the rod came down in the closet, dropping all the clothes on the floor and order had to be restored. You convicted me through supernatural prodding and I recognized this as Your handiwork and surrendered to it. I felt estranged from You because of my procrastination with this assignment. After I obeyed You, I slept like a baby last night! Thanks!!

"My #1 Is Still My #1!"

10/9/02

Lord,

As I fellowship with You, I realize that I am still harboring unforgiviness towards the people at my old church that has grown to include the members who were even there for me financially when I was being exploited by the church leaders. I curse this bitterness down to the root and ask You to exchange this spirit for one of love, kindness and forgiveness. I want it up and out of me so that I can have a clean heart to serve You! Help me rid myself of this destructive, unforgiving spirit. I confess Your Word daily over me, that greater is He who is in me (Holy Ghost) than he (devil) that is in this world. Holy Ghost, I give You total reign and authority to evict the trespassing spirits in me, *God's Property!!*

10/13/02

Lord,

No sooner than I confessed my need of Your help to loose my unforgiving spirit and bitterness, and You did it! I felt the weight of the grudge on my emotional health and needed deliverance. I realized on Friday that You did it! As I was talking to a friend of the family, I realized that hurt and anger didn't accompany the recitation of what the church leaders did to me. That was fast! I prayed and solicited prayer support on my behalf and **You did it again!** I am still studying Your Word and praying for myself as I continue in this healing process. Thank You, Jesus for being my balm in Gilead!!

I gave Kevin and Naomi's boxed clothes to Laverne for safe keeping. Kevin's family can go through his things to claim sentimental items and the leftovers will be made into a quilt for me and Miriam!!!

10/19/02

Lord,

You allow me to experience things for a season then it's time to move on to the next season or level You have planned for me. On this pilgrimage, I have multiple assignments to complete. I must remain available and sensitive to Your prodding and leading in order to be successful at doing what You have created me to do. Strengthen me Lord, as I process the revelation knowledge You have given me in regards to my healing process.

10/27/02

Lord,

I've been diligently working on myself and my understanding of forgiveness. This weekend, I experienced another emotional breakthrough! On Friday, I met You at a revival service at Southwest Community Church, *"The Bridge,"* where You prophesied through Your servant, George Bloomer, that I was healed from an incident that occurred at the age of eleven for me. He declared that I was (am) emotionally matured to my chronological age of thirty-eight from the age of eleven.

I was trying hard to figure out what in the world he was referring to that occurred in my childhood and what came to me was the spirit of rejection that came about through my Dad. He rejected me because of my independent spirit from his domineering, oppressive behaviors due to his alcoholism. I guess the spirit of rejection grew from the seed that was planted inside of me by my Dad when I suffered subsequent losses, disappointments, and rejections as life went on.

The tragic experience of my family's accident had brought me back emotionally to age eleven when I had to begin doing for and protecting myself. I realized at that age that people will let you down. Even those you should be able to count on to support you like my Dad, then my husband, and my old church. ***Prophet Bloomer called that spirit of rejection out of me and I became free!! Hallelujah, I'm free!!***

I also went to *"Flo's Kids Learning to Forgive"* Forgiveness Conference on Saturday hosted by Dr. Victoria J. Sloan, Clinical Psychologist, that picked up where the revival left off on Friday night. The forgiveness workshops I attended walked me through the process of working through this issue of forgiveness of my old church members as well as the church leaders. It brought to light the realization that I still needed to forgive Kevin as well in regards to the church debacle and I needed to call it out for what it really was – disappointment! I was **very disappointed** that Kevin didn't bring up my being called into ministry before his death. *I had to ask myself, "Why he didn't go to bat for me?" I have concluded it was because he wanted the Pastorate more!* He really thought that he could manage me and my call into the ministry at home. We just couldn't let the church find out about my call into ministry because then he could lose his Pastorate over that (the leadership was against women in ministry) and he wasn't willing to take that chance.

He was tormented for this duplicity because I pressed him to share my calling with the church and he refused to and hid it from them instead. He redefined my ministry fruit and tried to play it off for the church leaders' sake every time the question of my being a minister came up. His decision to hide my calling rather than share it with the church cost him my respect for him. I lost trust in him and felt betrayed that he would acknowledge me privately but wouldn't own me publicly in ministry. He tried to cover up my call into ministry really well and promised me that this year 2002, he would let the church know about it. He just needed more time to ease them into accepting women being called into ministry.

This secret made me feel like the *"other woman"* to the church! Normally, it's the other way around for Pastors' families with the church being the other woman to the family relationship. Kevin couldn't tell the secret about my call into ministry to the church, but he could utilize my ministry gifts at home to his own advantage and benefit. I was only allowed to work behind the scenes doing administrative tasks, brainstorming ideas for sermon series, and plan workshops and retreats. I could give him counseling advice for the members, write our fasting journals, and do our entire curriculum writing for the bible studies. But he would not publicly acknowledge any of this as my contributions. Instead, he took the credit for himself! This was so that the leaders wouldn't suspect (per his reasoning) that I was a *"boot-legged"* minister. How absurd! Now that I reflect on it, **that was asinine!** But at the time, I willingly went along with the charade to keep peace at the church and at home.

"My #1 Is Still My #1!"

We didn't have any other major problems in our marriage except for this one which was a *constant struggle between us*. He didn't feel comfortable letting on how much I helped him out in the ministry and I wouldn't let up on him to get him to acknowledge my ministry contributions publicly. When he would share something I had done for the church, he would do so begrudgingly. With such a reluctant attitude, I didn't care to hear about it then. It took too much effort and coaxing to get any acknowledgement out of him. Then, it was tempered as much as possible, so as not to make the leaders think he was complementing his wife too much publicly and giving her too much credit for contributing to the ministry at the church. *(I know, I know, so-o-o sad, but true!)*

In his defense, he did get much better in publicly recognizing my contributions to the ministry and telling the church how much he loved me, **the last six months before his death**! *I wonder if my speaking out at other churches softened his stance as he listened to the feedback from those ministries after I preached. He even began speaking out more about women in ministry in his sermons. But he never got a chance to come out of the closet publicly about my being called into the ministry before he died though. Selah.*

The other thing that I had to admit, for what it was, is *the fact that I was angry at the members who stayed at the church* even though they claimed to be in support of me and Miriam. Their remaining at the church after everything that happened was like a betrayal, as well as another disappointment to me. They agreed in theory about how badly I was treated by the church leaders, yet *they remained at the church that treated me so badly!* **No one but You, Jesus, was by my side! No one, but You! Hallelujah!**

The last thing that was painful for me to accept was when one of the church leaders told me privately that he believed women can be called into ministry and that he had no problem with me being called. **Yet he denied me - like Kevin did - when polled publicly** regarding his opinion on women ministers! This particular church leader "said" he was in support of me privately on many issues concerning the church drama, but came out against me publicly over, and over, again! This was the proverbial knife twisted in my chest. ***I was NOT going through this mess again! This man WASN'T my*** *husband (this time around) and I needed to get to an exit door out of there quick and FAST!!*

When I realized how many people (Kevin, church members, and church leaders) I was dragging behind me on this three-fold cord of unforgiveness, bitterness and anger, I really had to take inventory. I chose to release each and every one of them so that I could be free to latch on to the future You have for me without all of this unforgiveness blocking me! And as soon as I intentionally released them all in forgiveness of their offenses towards me, I felt relieved, lightened and refocused again! I could think more clearly to write again - *I am writing again!*

I could let go of my bitterness, anger (now that it was identified) and unforgiveness because none of those people were worth me losing out on my destiny with You and I had to clean out my heart! I only have so much room in it and I want to fill it up with Your Holy Spirit and Your Fruit of the Spirit! All of those people were human, frail, and had their own weaknesses. Again, You ALONE are my SOURCE, God! My only SOURCE, my dependable, faithful, comforting SOURCE!! Thank You, thank You, thank You, for this emotional breakthrough!

10/28/02

God, thank You for helping me to understand that You anointed Kevin with Your grace to endure Pastoring that hostile church where we were assigned. Your grace was sufficient for both of us to remain in such an unsupportive environment. When Kevin died, the anointing lifted and I had a very difficult time remaining in that place. I left hoping I could return one day, but I now realize beyond a shadow of a doubt that You only gave me grace to endure the loss of my husband and daughter, **not** to remain in a hostile church environment. *That is the reason why I can gracefully move through this grief journey, but could not tolerate, nor endure that negative, toxic, church environment any longer. The foul, evil spirits that took up residence over there made me sick to my stomach every time I was in their wicked presence.*

God promised me that *I would not go out empty!* God saw Kevin and I working for measly crumbs, He saw me being mistreated after Kevin's death, He saw the church leaders abuse their authority in regards to Kevin and me. Kevin died working in faith, not receiving his reward on this side, but I remain with Miriam and because of the Favor of God, *I will walk out of this oppressive situation with tremendous FAVOR.* Men <u>will give</u> unto me; pressed down, shaken together and running over will they give unto my bosom and to Miriam. We will inherit Kevin and Naomi's portion and our children's children down to four generations will still be spending this wealth transfer. The devil will repay us seven times for what he stole from my family. I will inherit what the Bible promised! The devil owes me seven times what I lost! God said when a thief is found out, that's what he owes me! I didn't just walk away from my old church freed from the yolk of their oppression, but I walked out with tremendous FAVOR and wealth, Hallelujah!

At the Potter's wheel, as God was forming me as a pot, He decided to make me into a beautiful vase instead. He pulled it up to reshape it and the vase (me) thought (I) would break under the pressure. He put the vase (me) in the fiery furnace to get rid of all the impurities of selfishness, sin, and iniquity in the clay (flesh). After it rises to the surface and is finished, (after a season), the potter moves it (the vase) out of the fire to another place to allow it (me) to cool off. After being in the fire in preparation for the glaze (releasing of anger, bitterness, unforgiviness from fiery trials), He then decides where He will place the vase (me). It has to be a high place to display His Glory, for others to see His working through me. God's looking for a high place to display His trophies for others to look to for hope, and for their own restoration as well.

Lord, I finally have to admit that I was embarrassed by the way the church leaders treated me after Kevin died. I couldn't believe their lack of love openly displayed towards the Pastor's family. I thought they would at least behave better towards me on this occasion. Many people were watching and the church leaders didn't treat me any better than they had treated us privately at the church when

"My #1 Is Still My #1!"

Kevin was alive. The church leadership disrespected him as their Pastor, they had no regard for his family, they paid him poorly and refused to give him a raise even though the church could afford to do so, they stole his money from him on his installation day as Pastor, they didn't give him anything when his daughter (Miriam) was born, they couldn't come together to plan for a birthday or Christmas gift for him, nor plan his first year anniversary program. All of this abuse and mistreatment we suffered silently, but ***You God saw it all and will reward me openly!***

The whole Christian community in Houston got to see how ill-treated we were by the church leadership and their "laundry" was out! They blamed me for it, but Your Word says that what's done in secret will be shouted from the roof top! ***And so it was!*** Their hearts were never changed! The pop quiz on their faith level by tests and trials came up again and their grade didn't change from the last time they had FLUNKED! *I pray that I passed!!* Every thing I studied these past four years as I served at the church came back to me, *along with the fact that it's an open book test with the Bible! **Duh!***

I look back on the medical leave I had to take in 2000 when I stayed home on bed rest during my challenging pregnancy with Miriam and remember how I fed my spirit with the Word of God for nine months. That season allowed me to stack my spirit up and top off my inner man in preparation for this season when *my spiritual root system had to go down DEEP in order to stand and after all I did **to continue to stand**! **I know** it was because of that season that I was prepared for this season!* I have frequently reminisced on the spiritual experiences I had at Windsor Village UMC as a prayer warrior, going to their women's retreats, listening to their Bible teachers, and guest speakers. I consider all of that as the spiritual training I needed in order to endure this harsh season of testing. Those experiences taught me what I needed to do to get out of the pit of despair when I landed in it. They taught me how to audibly speak my healing, deliverance, and faith into existence! *Spiritual Warfare is **FOR REAL** and it is for keeps!* I need to remember who the real enemy is (Satan) and remain focused, sober-minded, and vigilante as a soldier on the battlefield. Thank You, Lord!

What I have found out about myself during this trial is that I had to do battle for myself, <u>while</u> soliciting intercessory prayer to have the strength to endure. I had to use all of my weapons of warfare: prayer, praise, worship and giving to bring Your Presence into my trial to torment the enemy rather than have the enemy torment me in this trial. I also found out that *I knew <u>how to use</u> my weapons of warfare and that they <u>were effective</u> to pulling down every stronghold that rose up against me! I took them captive to the authority and in the Name of Jesus, as my daily spiritual discipline!*

Kevin's job was to preach the Word at the church; my job was to walk alongside him. He carried out his assignment until his death and my assignment ended when he died. I'm beginning to better understand that assignment and its season. My head and heart are on the same page regarding that matter now. The workshops I attended this weekend were the antidote that opened up my eyes to see what this spiritual warfare really was about. *You were who we served in that church and who we answered to. I overstayed my assignment by staying three months after Kevin's death. That's when strife came into the church and carnality ruled where You used to reign when Kevin was the Pastor. The church became dysfunctional immediately and the craziness from the chaos was driving me to insanity. Hallelujah, I knew when to get off of the little short bus!* (Smile)

It became very apparent that my spiritual health was at stake and I needed to make a decision: move forward, remain stagnant, or go backwards. *I chose to move forward* in another fellowship rather than stay where there was no opportunity to grow spiritually or work in ministry. I didn't want to go back to Egypt (spiritually dry place). I couldn't go back, I've come too far, to turn back now! Being away from my former church and visiting other ministries that were spiritually freer than them allowed me the time and space I needed to work on me.

I was no longer distracted by the church drama and could focus on my issues. In seeing about me and mine (Miriam), I realized that my spirit *and heart* needed to be cleaned out before I stepped into the next level that God has for me. I don't want to be promoted with animosity in my heart. I will be representing You and I don't want to misrepresent or tarnish Your image, Lord. So before I am elevated, *I must go through the process of brokenness to sanctify and prove myself before the next assignment You have for me.*

10/29/02

Lord,

I realize that I am in a season of having my heart attitude adjusted. My will has been submitted to Your will, but I needed to cleanse my heart in order to serve You without spot or blemish. I don't want to contaminate Your ministry with my unresolved issues!! I'm working on this area in preparation for my next level. I see clearly now that the fog has lifted through this weekend of self reflection.

The unseen, (to the natural eye), can linger for a long time undetected and unaddressed until the Holy Ghost shines a light on it! Amen!

NOVEMBER

11/1/02

Lord,

On last night You rehearsed with me the following truths that I had to grow emotionally and spiritually stronger in before I was able to handle them:

1. Kevin may have been intimidated by the calling on my life to ministry; he may have possibly thought he would have to compete with me, who knows?
2. Kevin wanted the Pastorate at the old church more than he wanted to support my being called into ministry.
3. Kevin accepted an abusive relationship with the church leaders; he wouldn't assert himself, nor stand up against their selfishness towards him and our family.
4. Kevin's acquiescence to the leadership, for the sake of becoming Pastor of the old church, may have shortened his life (Deuteronomy 29:29 states that the secret things belong to the Lord and are a wonder to us).

I called the acquiescence giving in to bullying because Kevin wouldn't believe that God could protect the Pastorate for him if he came out publicly in support of me in ministry or if he spoke up for himself against their abuses. He never spoke up for himself or the family about their mistreatment of us. He eventually began preaching that God could use women, but he still avoided coming out saying God could use me – *his wife!* He resisted for some reason or another to support me and his silence on the matter for two years had to be reconciled (by me) after his death.

I know beyond a shadow of a doubt that the devil **customized this evil** to take me out. My family of origin was in a tragic accident – Dad died instantly, Mom subsequently, Charlotta and Jeanette survived. Kevin, Naomi, and Miriam were in a tragic accident - Kevin died instantly, Naomi subsequently, and Miriam survived. The same tragedy, different family! The difference this time around was my response - I was wiser and better. I was spiritually armed and ready to use my weapons of warfare to navigate the mine fileds of this tragedy and walk out on the other side victorious in King Jesus!

THIS time around, I was thanking Him for my healing and the strength to endure this fiery trial before I even realized that I was in the greatest spiritual battle of my short life. What I found out about myself this time around was that I knew more spiritually than I gave myself credit for. I was spiritually matured enough to recognize what was really going on and **I remembered** how to utilize my weapons for spiritual warfare. I realize now that both of these tragedies were spiritual warfare attacks on my faith. They were designed by Satan to take me out, put me off-task, and not focus on my position in God's Army. My destiny is still as secure as it was before time and I *will fulfill* my purpose!

I forgive Kevin for his frailty, he always wanted to be a Pastor and he died in that office. I on the other hand want to go down in *God's Spiritual Book of Faith as a living epistle read by men*, not a particular title such as reverend, or Pastor. I want to leave a spiritual legacy for this generation and future generations to draw strength from when their faith is tested in their trials by fire - Hallelujah!! And, I can't leave this earth until that happens!

Possible theme Scripture and title for my book about this trial, "But God," Psalm 34:19 *"Many are the afflictions of the righteous, but the Lord rescues us from them all."*

THE TRUTHS THAT *I NOW* KNOW:

I was postponed spiritually by my own compromise with Kevin at the church to be silent about my calling into ministry. I worked behind the scenes as directed, nevertheless, You, God, saw everything. You tested the motives of my heart to see if I could be trusted.

The enemy is trying to stop me because of what tomorrow holds, not because of what yesterday held. The battle is not over my past, it's over my future! The battle is for my future harvest, and the greater the battle, the greater my future!

11/8/02

3:15 A.M.

Lord, Lord, Lord, I keep waking up and I can't go back to sleep!

I've been meditating on why I've been awakened at this hour and all I can think of is how Miriam woke up on yesterday, her 23 months birthday, saying, "my sister" very clearly articulated. She continued repeating it over, and over, and over, all the way to school. Then, when we returned home, she continued to amaze me by saying, "Naomi," like someone was coaching her to say it to me. I asked her who was Naomi and she pointed to Nne's picture over the fireplace!

Where did that come from, Lord?! I haven't talked about Naomi for a while. Miriam's preoccupation with her sister on her 23 months birthday, 11/7/02, was too much of a coincidence for me. So, I asked Miriam who was she talking to and she said, "My sister, Naomi!" I asked her was she talking to her right now and she said <u>yesh</u>!! (Mmi's yes for now!) I left it alone.

I know we live in a three dimensional world and the spirit world operates in our physical world, but I know that dead people don't come back. I know that God allows angels to carry messages to us from heaven. I don't want to get sentimental, but what does this experience mean, Lord? I'm pressing on towards my destiny on this earth. I want to get through this trial so that I can be about Your business. Is this "Naomi Rhetoric" just another distraction? Help me to continue to think clearly and soberly on these matters!

11/16/02

Lord,

Last night was heart wrenching for me! It was as if Your Spiritual Hand came into my heart and squeezed it like a towel to release my tears of sorrow. My tears flowed like liquid prayers for six hours. The more I released, the more I had to release. I cried from the prayer room, to the bedroom, to the great room, to the bathroom. All of these places now have stains from my tears.

I was tired, just absolutely fed up with having to come home to an empty house and having to deal with caring for Miriam all alone! I needed to know You hadn't forgotten about me, and allow You to hear me cry out in frustration and just sob!! Deep, from the belly sobs, gut-wrenching, snot producing cries about this transition of season that I am in. I was simply tired and frustrated by it all!

Grief is very lonely and magnified for me because Miriam is so young. She's not able to reciprocate caretaking of Mommy, like Mommy does for her. I miss Kevin and Naomi and time still marches forward without them.

All I can think about lately is Thanksgiving last year and Jeanette's visit because she had a feeling she needed to come and spend that time with us. Then, not more than two months later, that feeling or better described as the *unction of the Holy Spirit,* was revealed through the tragedy of Kevin and Naomi's deaths. We are coming up on the holidays, New Year's, and the one year anniversary of their deaths.

HELP ME, LORD!
PLEASE, COMFORT ME LIKE YOU DID right after the accident!
ANESTHETIZE ME to make it through these holidays!
PLEASE, PLEASE, PLEASE, PLEASE! <u>PLEASE</u>!!

My neck and shoulders had been tight and aching the latter part of this week. I needed to relax, so I tried prayer, praise, confession, and wound up having to take my meds again to help lower my anxiety level. I had no idea that my anxiety level was so high. It caused me to grind my teeth at night which caused headaches, jaw pain, and neck pain. I think its TMJ. It's just now starting to subside since I took the Xanax. Will I need to take meds to make it through the holidays? Only You know, Lord!

Miriam is so happy, cheerful, and loving. She is the angel that helps me to push forward. She's my motivation to continue to press toward my healing. I want to do it for her so when she begins to ask me details about her Dad and sister I can answer her freely without bitterness and unresolved issues. Kevin was human, with frailties and faults like all other mortal men, but God used him mightily in preaching and teaching His Word! Naomi was an obedient child, and a scholarly student with a wonderful personality. They will forever be a part of Miriam's and my lives even in their absence. I am confident that they have gone on ahead of us to heaven to prepare our mansions and that Miriam and I will be along shortly (when eternity is the time frame).

Lord, Lord, Lord, Lord, Lord, comfort me! Keep me, my mind, and my thoughts on You!

11/18/02

Tonight, Lord, You allowed me to share my testimony publicly for the *first* time (with Mia holding my hand, standing by my side) at The Fountain of Praise's Women's Fellowship. The anointing on me was awesome as I continued to minister to the women in small groups throughout the evening. You used me at the back of the church and in the parking lot after tonight's fellowship. The women were blessed by **Your strength** displayed in me!!

I told them the reason for my strength was that *"My #1 Is Still My #1!!"* You Alone, God! You Alone, are the reason!! It got them to thinking to themselves about how they have to get some things in order, to rearrange their priorities after hearing my testimony. I'm also thinking that phrase *"My #1 Is Still My #1!!"* would be a great title for the book.

11/22/02

Yeah! I made it through this week! I had a hard time because of tiredness and weariness but with Your help, I made it! I bathed Miriam, put her down to sleep and began cooking our Thanksgiving meal tonight. Cooking is very therapeutic for me. I made gumbo, dirty rice, wild rice, stuffed bell peppers and my feet got tired from standing up in the kitchen for so long. I'll cook the greens and macaroni and cheese tomorrow morning. I took out our smoked turkey meat that I had frozen earlier this month and that will complete our Thanksgiving meal. I will freeze half of the Thanksgiving meal for Christmas and begin eating the other half this weekend. I was looking forward to this weekend for the rest and relaxation and I'm hoping to get that too!

I'm restless, ambivalent and anxious about the holidays. I plan to volunteer at the George R. Brown Convention Center on Thanksgiving Day feeding the homeless, to help keep my mind off of myself. I think that by keeping busy, I won't have to think about how I spent last Thanksgiving with Kevin, Naomi, Jeanette, Earl, and Miriam. This year it will be me and Miriam at my mother-in-law's after I work at the convention center.

Lord, only You know all about my troubles!

You alone, God, know the emotions I am going through and the drama I'm trying to keep to a minimum in regards to the old church recognizing Kevin as their late Pastor before the end of this year. My in-laws are pushing for a proper recognition ceremony for Kevin from the church. Nothing has materialized as of yet for him, even though the church leaders promised me that they would do something back in May when we talked before I left the church.

After reading this book titled "*A Life God Rewards,*" I am convinced that Bruce Wilkerson has the right perspective on things. Kevin and Naomi are already in their reward. They are in eternity where I long to join them and my other loved ones (shortly) when You send for me. I figure in my due season, after I have completed the assignment You have given me, I can go home to heaven for my own reward. Hallelujah!

Just continue to keep me, direct me, heal me, and comfort me, Lord! When I feel that I am being kept, directed, healed, and comforted I can go on a little while longer to see what my end will be. Help me to run on King Jesus! Lead me to the Rock that is higher than I.

The perspective I received from Bruce Wilkerson's book, *"A Life God Rewards,"* really helped me to put my own life into perspective. Everything I do will have a subsequent consequence in heaven. I need to make sure I have stored up my treasures there for when I follow along behind them. My treasure goes first, and then I follow my treasure. What I don't know is how long will it be before my heart follows my head? I've scheduled some me time for next week, a spa sampler and a counseling session for Monday. Let's see if that helps me to get closer to closing the gap (again) between my heart and my head.

11/23/02

Lord,

I'm still tired and exhausted! Mmi has been up since 6 A.M. I went to sleep around 12 A.M. She's been active all morning, now she's whining! I need a break! I am casting this care on You! I need a break that doesn't take me two to three days to recuperate from due to having to nurse Mmi back to health after being *"cared for"* by well meaning family and friends. The last two to three times she's been cared for by others she came back sick, which is of no help to me if I have to use all my energies recouped from resting, spent on taking care of her (again). I could just keep her home with me for that matter; it's feels like the same benefit (none) to me.

Now my neck is tense, my head is hurting, and I'm tired!! **Help Me!** I cry unto You, Lord! I'm not on the phone whining to other people. **I cry to You and I EXPECT *You* to come and see about me!** I expect You to send me some GOOD HELP! I will lend my body on Thanksgiving as a servant at the convention center to be used by You in service to others, who will yield themselves to be of service as a babysitter for me on Your behalf? **HELP!!**

I finished cooking the baked macaroni and greens to complete our Thanksgiving meal this morning. I went to the store and bought key lime pie for dessert and White Zinfandel to complement the meal. Everything tastes delicious! Thank You, Lord that I am here to cook, taste and enjoy this meal! Miriam doesn't like anything more than the dirty rice so far. I am still spiritually dry! I began watching video tapes to help me through this dry spell. I'm anxiously anticipating the upcoming holidays and can't stay focused on today, where I am! Help me to not borrow from tomorrow's trouble!

God, You showed me on last Sunday that my old church is definitely dead to me. The Women of Standard Ministry invited me to dinner last weekend to present me with a plaque for my service to the church and for leading the Women's Ministry. I wasn't even moved or touched by their gesture. I accepted their award graciously (without any tears) and realized that I had already moved on emotionally. The plaque's in the room with the rest of the award presentations for Nne and me. I realized when I got home that *I'm dead even to my dearest ministry from the old church* – **The Women of Standard.** Through the Power of Your Healing Word, my soul ties to the old church are broken, it's over! Hallelujah! Thank You, Jesus, for showing me that the emotional ties are cut to my old church!! You are faithful, yet AGAIN! Yes!!

I wrote a letter earlier this week on behalf of the family to request that the leadership at the old church finally acknowledge Kevin's contributions to the church by the deadline of 12/22/02. I told Laverne that if they don't do it by then, let us all then as a family move on emotionally from a church that once meant so much to us. As of today, we haven't heard anything back from the church leaders.

My special assignment at the old church ended when Kevin died. My four year tour of duty as a soldier in the Army of the Lord assigned over there is up and I have been on spiritual furlough ever since. I finally understand that *I lent my body to YOU for four years*

"My #1 Is Still My #1!"

of service at that church. Now that I know my old church is DEAD to me, I can move forward and stop looking back into my past.

Now, I have reported for duty in my new assignment as the Chairperson of The Christian Development Center (CDC) at Kainos Community Church. This assignment seems like it, too, will be challenging. The CDC at this church includes the nursery, preschool, Wednesday night Bible study, and Sunday morning classes. As the Chairperson, I am expected to recruit and train teachers for the classes, hold monthly teachers' meetings, maintain class attendance logs, and come up with Bible study series ideas. *Whew, I'm tired just writing out all of those responsibilities!*

Next year, I had planned on taking two distance learning classes from Trinity Theological Seminary towards my Doctorate in Religious Studies (DRS). I still have my professional duties as an Assistant Principal at two elementary schools, as well as being a single Mom to little Miriam, OK!? Lord, You really have some serious undergirding to do for me in 2003! My goals are real ambitious for this next year!

God's prophesies over me for 2003 are:

1. *Everyplace that the sole of my feet tread, God said He has given to me!*
2. *Things and places that I have touched, God said is for me! Not for somebody else!*
3. *When God gets ready to bless me, no man or woman shall be able to stand against me all the days of my life!*
4. *No weapon formed against me shall prosper!*

Hallelujah to His Name! Jesus! I receive that!

11/28/02

Lord,

From meditation and prayer I see two books that are ready to be birthed. *"But God"* will be my autobiography of life from childhood in an alcoholic home to the present, and *"My #1 Is Still My #1!"* will be my testimony book from this year's, 1/31/02, experience.

The responses I have received from sharing my testimony have been tremendous and eye opening for me. I took my ability to rebound from this tragedy for granted. I assumed that everyone had the same priorities as I did when it came to You first, spouse second, and children third. What I found so remarkable was that **many have their priorities out of balance** *and that is why they are amazed by how I have the strength to continue to go on.*

Now, I see more clearly the anointed power of my **"Keep on, keeping on, in spite of everything I'm coming though"** attitude. I need to share with others how I kept on keeping on when everything around me had fallen apart, or *in my case burned up!*

My faith in You God has carried me through and will continue to carry me on. I have deepened my experience and knowledge base of Your Sovereignty, Your keeping Power, and Your Healing Power as Jehovah Rapha - my emotional healer - Hallelujah! This grief journey sent my root system deeper into **Your WORD!!** It's all I had to carry me to this point of my testimony. I couldn't opt out, nor jump in and out at will. **I had to walk this thing out daily, with God to help me, because it is <u>MY TESTIMONY</u>!**

You allowed my family and friends to come along side me at Your discretion and on Your timing and schedule and for that I thank You! Also, I thank You that You helped me to realize that I was bitter because some people weren't consistently there for me throughout my journey and that *You arranged it to be so.* This grief journey is TOO MUCH for some people to bear, even alongside me, so I let them off the hook. **You sent who You wanted to send! You elevated those who needed to be raised up to come alongside me to share in this** *extremely heavy* **emotional load.**

God, I truly thank You for this support! It has totally eased my emotional stress levels. Again, I give You all the PRAISE!! You have peeled me (like an onion) out of many layers of grave clothes and I am being loaded up daily with the benefits from being submitted to You. Spiritual understanding, revelation knowledge, wisdom and peace are just a few of the things that I can easily recall receiving as a result of this grief journey.

Serving dinner at the Convention Center on Thanksgiving Day accomplished what I wanted it to do. It kept my mind off of myself and numbed me through fatigue so that when I got home, I was too exhausted to have a "pity party." I got a chance to clear my mind as I did the repetitive work of serving plate after plate after plate of food to others. The hard work was good for my soul today.

11/29/02

Lord,

    I didn't plan on it, but You arranged today to be the day for me to clean out the garage, Nne's room, Mmi's room, and the girls' playroom. My sister-in-law, Charolette, came by to put air in my work dolly's tires and then one thing led to another. We began cleaning the house, cleaning the garage, cleaning Nne's room, and MY TEARS began rolling down UNCONTROLLABLY! The tears came on me so strong, I couldn't stop crying!!

    I boo-hooed the whole time we were in Nne's room as she took out her furniture to the garage. Just the act of changing Nne's room out to the exercise room knocked the wind out of me. I was knocked down for at least an hour from cleaning because of it. Now her room has my tear stains in it as well. We finally completed converting it to the exercise room. It isn't her room anymore and she is not coming back to claim it. I placed all of my exercise equipment in the room along with the floor model TV and VCR. The room is completely redone now. All that is needed are the wall decorations and drapes.

    I also reorganized the play room. I took out all of Nne's things and put them in the garage. Now the play room only has Mmi's things in it and books galore. I put up Nne's memorabilia on the wall. I need to buy a few more items to even out the décor for that room.

    I purchased a HDTV for the family room to complete that room. All I need are the draperies to completely redecorate the family room, my bedroom, and the bath. Now, I can move on to refurnishing Miriam's bedroom. I would have totally redecorated the house by the *first* anniversary of their deaths next year and everything in it will look completely different. This will help me to not fall into a deeper depression as I rehearse memories of them because I would have created new ones with every decision I made in home redecorating. I will only have to keep up with the house cleaning after this, *along with keeping up with Miriam.*

Miriam makes two years old next week, 12/07/02, next Saturday. So much has happened since her first birthday...

DECEMBER

12/3/02

Today was *"Holiday Meltdown Day"* for me. We are only five days into the holiday season and I'm ready to hide out until after February 14th. I had a meltdown early this morning on the way to work and never made it in. I called out for help and my friend Dr. Carolyn Clansy, Clinical Psychologist, answered my S.O.S., as well as my coworker at school. Mary Garza, my school counselor, kept me on the phone talking until Carolyn was able to physically come to comfort me as I stood on the side of the road. Both tried to comfort me while I processed the emotions that were overwhelming to me at the time. I felt like I was drowning. I couldn't breathe and I couldn't see for all of my tears.

What had triggered this panic attack was seeing my OB/GYN this morning. He didn't know that Kevin and Naomi had passed away in January. When he asked about them and I told him what had happened, he took it really hard, along with his nurse. He couldn't believe that he didn't know about the accident and their deaths after all of this time, and he was in shock. **Because today was Day One for them, their strong emotional reactions to the news brought me back to Day One of my fiery trial!**

He delivered Naomi and Miriam and was very close to Kevin. He never knew that they had died earlier this year and it took the wind out of him when he found out. He could hardly complete my exam. It was real sad for them to find out that way, but it was crushing for me to see them so hurt. I empathized with him and it pained me so strongly that I thought I had regressed and felt as though I was drowning in *his* sea of sorrow. It overwhelmed me and I had to save myself!! I had fought too long and hard these past few months to stay afloat and I felt that I was sinking because of his sorrow and grief. Add to that, the grieving that my sister-in-law is sharing with me as she processes her own feelings after helping me to clear out Naomi's room and I'm going down with the heaviness of OTHER *people's sorrows over their grief and loss of Kevin and Naomi.* **Help!** I can't handle it!

It's enough to keep myself afloat during this stressful time of year and they are not helping me! My counselor said I should make a list of those persons I need to limit my contact with this time of year so that I can successfully navigate through the emotional days ahead. I need Your wisdom and strength, Lord, even more so or as much as I needed it in February of this year. It's already a difficult season for me emotionally. The "white knuckle" anxiety of trying to keep it together in spite of societal pressures, cultural expectations, and constant questions on "How was your holiday?" from well meaning folks is ***enough already!!*** Five days into the holiday season and I already want out of this stressful time of year. I consented to go back on meds to make it through this long season of the holidays, Miriam and my birthdays and the upcoming *first* year anniversary of the accident on January 31st! This is all too much for me to digest and I want to get away and hibernate from it all – alone!

This is one of the ways I can cope with the anxiety and depression that has crept up on me. Already, I felt relief as I took the Xanax after my panic attack on today. It mellowed me out and managed my crisis enough to allow me to go to sleep today, (even though I'm up now at 2:20 A.M. writing). I pray my sleep schedule will become regulated once I get my emotional stability back.

12/9/02

Thank God, I made it through last week ***and*** Miriam's second birthday! We had parties at her school on Friday and at home on Saturday to celebrate her second birthday. They also sang "Happy Birthday" to her on Sunday at Children's Church as well. I struggled with my emotions most of the week. But, God! You strengthened me over the weekend and I am still here! I overcame my feelings of anxiety with personal prayer and intercessory prayer support. Today was a better day for me and I made it through the day. Hallelujah!

I decided to pray up and prepare to attend the memorial and appreciation for Kevin & Naomi this week at my old church. They *finally* responded to our request. I really need Your strength to make it through this last test of faith and for patience during this very stressful season. As I see things more clearly now, I realize that I will be participating in a new members graduation ceremony at my new church, Kainos Community Church, on the same date that my old church planned the memorial service for Kevin. That date will be promotion at one place and closure at another - *a very emotional day, indeed!*

12/13/02

Lord,

I got such a simple revelation today while driving and it was this: If I could forgive Kevin for disregarding my calling, not openly accepting me in ministry and putting me on the shelf until he got back to me - why couldn't I forgive the church leaders? They only did openly what their Pastor did privately to me and I allowed him to do it. That's why I was bound and determined not to waste another day over there. I was sat down for two years until Kevin could get back to me and all of my anger and rage came up and out at them because I wasn't even taken seriously by my **OWN husband**!

Kevin and I argued often about this issue and it constantly caused a wedge between us. I don't know if Kevin was threatened by my calling or why he wouldn't acknowledge it publicly. I resented it then and after his death I wouldn't sit back and wither away any longer. I wanted to be acknowledged as a called out minister and gave the church leaders the opportunity to accept or reject my calling and was infuriated that they chose to table it like Kevin did. I accepted it from him because he was my husband but I wasn't going to sit and wait around again, *not this time!* It was *his choice* to join our family with that church and now he was dead. The old church became dead to me as well because of their "let's sit and wait it out" stance. I needed to get out of a stifling and suffocating spiritual environment for my own survival. For me, it was matter of spiritual life or death and **I chose LIFE –** *the life more abundantly that <u>Christ died for me to have</u>*!!!

Kevin died and left me at a church that was not on the same page spiritually with me and I had to leave and find a fellowship where the issue of women in ministry was already settled. Kevin was their leader and they were acting the same way he had with me and I was *livid* that I was experiencing rejection from them (like Kevin) on top of dealing with my family losses. Why couldn't we heal together, grow in spiritual maturity together and get through this fiery trial together? They turned against me, rejected me and refused to support me! The same things Kevin was guilty of in regards to my vocational ministry.

I remember the day that I spoke at a Women's Conference, 7/31/01, where I was the Keynote Speaker and how rude Kevin was throughout my speaking engagement by hand signaling me to wrap it up. Thank God, I didn't pay him any mind and flowed with the Spirit until You completed Your message through me. But it reminded me that the church leaders were emulating the behavior of their late leader. **I <u>had</u> to let them off the hook!** I constantly had to forgive Kevin for his insensitivity towards me when I ministered to others. He never equated what I did as being as significant to the Kingdom as to what he did when ministering to others. I had to call him out in order to get ANY recognition for doing the same things that he would go overboard thanking any of the church leaders for doing at the church.

He would tell me that because I was more spiritually mature than them, I could handle not being recognized publicly and I should give him a break because of all the hell he had to put up with from the church leaders. He pulled that trump card on me and I backed off, because I knew he was catching hell from them, but I was still hurt by his actions. And because I never got to process my hurt feelings, but only stuffed them deep down inside of me, I was overwrought with anger towards the leaders' "spiritual abuse" of me. I never realized it until now as I am writing this that it was because

"My #1 Is Still My #1!"

their response reminded me of the way I felt oppressed by Kevin's own "spiritual abuse" of me. He benefited from my insights, teachings, and skills, but wouldn't give me credit for anything I did for him and we argued constantly about that behind the scenes. I guess I realized that I didn't have to take spiritual abuse from anyone, anymore, after he was dead and I was free to make my own spiritual decisions again. That's when I knew I would leave the old church, I just didn't know when, but I knew I was out of there for sure!

It was when I started visiting other churches that I could breathe again. Visiting other churches reminded me of when **I had to supplement my church attendance before** when we attended spiritually dead churches that Kevin chose for us as a family to join. I had to keep my spirit alive until you, God, would deliver me to my season to fulfill my own destiny and that season is <u>NOW</u>! Thank you, Jesus! Lord, that simple revelation revealed a pattern of me biding my time until I could be free to make my own decisions. It was the same for me at home with my Dad, then I married a man who later reminded me of my Dad when he oppressed my spiritual gifting. What wonderful insight from personal reflection, thanks!

Kevin wasn't always spiritually oppressive. We came out of and were married at a church that had women Pastors on staff. After we married, he felt called to Pastor his own church and became obsessed with getting a Pastorate. The more he interviewed for Pastor at local churches, the more he was rejected for one reason or another.

One church called him back to offer him the Pastorate after their first choice of Pastor declined their offer. I asked him to pray before giving them an answer and he and I talked it over after he prayed and agreed that he should pass on their offer as well, after more information about the church came to light. When he called them back, he also declined their offer. Later on when he talked it over with some of his minister friends, they convinced him that he had made the wrong decision after talking it over with me and they urged him to call the church back to accept their offer to Pastor them. When he called to accept their offer, they informed him that they had moved on to their third choice.

After this incident, he vowed to never allow me to deter him from a Pastorate again because *I counseled him not to take that Pastorate* in Houston. From then on, he would be making all the spiritual decisions for himself and he didn't care what I shared with him that God had revealed to me about our spiritual decisions. He was going to answer for his own decisions. So stubbornness became a stronghold in him and he wouldn't allow my calling into the ministry to cost him the Pastorate at the old church. He would remind me often of how I cost him a Pastorate before and if he listened to me again I would cost him this one too. After that rebuke, I closed my mouth and waited for God to work it out for me.

God KNEW the type of oppressive environment that HE called me out of to minister His Word, just like I knew, and wondered why in the world He (God) would do this to me. I had to be silent and wait to see how He (God) was going to work this out for me. In the meantime, I submitted to my Pastor (Kevin) and served him in any and every capacity he needed and kept my mouth shut. People who know me personally, know how difficult that was for me to do because of my personality, and can not believe that I cosigned to do such a thing. But, *I realized that this was a God thing* and I had to stay in my lane by submitting to spiritual authority(my husband and Pastor) in order to allow Him (God) to do what He was going to do in this situation. I made my peace with the situation and accepted things for the way they were for that season of my calling.

Kevin controlled the information about my call to ministry and if I wanted peace in our house, I had to leave the decision of the right timing to tell the church about it to him. He said he knew when they would be ready for such news and he would decide when to tell them. I knew the church leaders made him sign a contract with a clause stating **he could not make any major changes at the church for the first three years as their Pastor** or his Pastorate would have been in jeopardy. The leaders would rescind their decision of making him their Pastor if he did make any changes and he couldn't risk that possibility, so that is why he closely guarded the information about my call to ministry.

Unfortunately, he never got around to telling them, even though he promised he was getting them ready this year, 2002, to accept women being called into ministry. He was scared to challenge them and didn't want to rock the boat. We were just getting steady this year and closing the gap between the "them" and "us" mentality. Kevin and I were beginning to believe that we were actually making headway with the church. Then the accident happened and everyone went back to their old cliques allowing factions and dissension to form in the church once again.

I challenge myself again with the question, if I forgave Kevin of his indifference towards me, why can't I forgive the church leaders? It really is that plain and simple and takes away the smoking guns. **I chose to forgive Kevin and I have to choose to forgive them as well.** It is finished, over and done with already, let's move on.

God and I are making my spiritual decisions now and I, alone, am accountable to Him! I have no husband to hide behind for bad discernment and bad decisions, it's on me now. It's up to me to make wise decisions for me and Miriam. I have to lean and depend on You, Lord, to lead me and guide me in the ways that I should go. You, Lord, will heal my broken heart with Your Word. You, God, will work all things together for my good because I am called according to Your purpose. You, God, are my Healer, my Comforter, and my Redeemer! You, God, are Jehovah! You, alone, know what You are doing in my life! Amen!

12/25/02

Lord,

God today is my 39th birthday! I have lived to see my birthday in the year, 2002! This year, we recognized Nne's and Kevin's birthdays without them. Earlier this month, we celebrated Mmi's birthday and now it's my turn! I have to constantly remind myself that just because Kevin and Naomi aren't here does not mean that there's no Christmas without them. ***There is no Christmas without You!***

It is definitely different this year. I woke up alone in my bedroom to Miriam letting me know she was up and ready to be fed breakfast. I got up and began our everyday routine. Charlotta's down here to help me make it through the day. She came to visit on Sunday and will leave out tomorrow when I leave for a visit to Connecticut. I've mainly been busy doing last minute things, but really "busy" as a distraction, more than anything else.

I went to the Christmas Eve Celebration at my new church last night and it was real nice, Christ centered and all. I thought of Naomi the whole time I saw the kids ministering through praise dance and singing on the program. I knew that Nne could have been right there with them and I missed being able to look at a children's program and see *"my"* baby perform. I made it through the program and made it home. Laverne, Sue, and Lloyd attended with me, Mmi, and Charlotta. This was the first time my family visited my new church with me and it felt nice to have guests attending.

10 A.M.

Today, I just want to sleep! I'm tired and possibly depressed and I don't want to be bothered right now. I've received two birthday calls so far and reluctantly took them. I don't feel like putting on a "face" to greet people today. Help me, Holy Ghost! You know the routine and You know I need a life preserver and it's in the Word! Teach me how to finish strong! I want to help me, too! I know I can make it through today, but I need a pep rally, not just a little talk with Jesus! I need a whole cheering section, not just me encouraging myself! Raise up cheerleaders as substitutes for my number one and number two cheerleaders being absent! I don't feel like my birthday is anything special for me this year. It just feels like any other day, with no special attention from my family to make up for Kevin and Nne's absence today.

I'm ready to go back to bed and wake up tomorrow in time to go on my get-a-way trip to Connecticut by way of New York City. It's time for me to get away from the family and parenting responsibilities. It's time for a little personal R&R to clear my head in order to move forward in my healing.

11 A.M.

Thank You for sending intercessory prayers directly to me. You ministered to me by moving Rev. and Sis Jackson (Mia's Mom and Dad) to call and check on me. They prayed with me to move this spirit of depression up and off of me! Up and off, in the Name of Jesus, Hallelujah!! I feel relieved and *can do* today now!

12 P.M.

Thank You for sending my brother-in-law, Wayne, over with gifts for me and Miriam. It cheered me up today to see that he remembered my birthday was on Christmas and gave me a gift of picture frames! Those frames will come in real handy, especially after all of the pictures I have taken of Miriam and me lately. Miriam received clothes, computer games, and a magna-doodle, she was so excited!

1 P.M.

Lord, You sent my next door neighbor, Mary, over to shower Miriam with more gifts. Her visit, remembering us on Christmas day was truly heart warming. Thank You! I have finished one of Bishop T.D. Jakes' videos on *"Don't Choke on Your Dreams"* and it really ministered to me, again! Bishop T.D. Jakes, Joyce Meyer, and Charles Stanley have really ministered to me along this journey through grief. Thank You for sending people to minister to me on today, You are the Lifter of My Head! Hallelujah!! Miriam is finally napping while Charlotta and I are resting.

3:30 P.M.

By this time, we were at my in-laws' family gathering for the holiday. I gave the family the Christmas tree ornament mementos that I had bought for everyone. *"Merry Christmas from heaven"* was on one side of it and the other side was inscribed with Kevin and Naomi's name with the year 2002. It was an emotional day for me, but I made it through, thank You, Jesus! You strengthened me, Lord, and *I made it* through! Before I left for the family gathering I stacked my soul with the Word of God from Bishop T.D. Jakes' tapes. They really encouraged me and helped me to gain the courage I needed to face the family this Christmas, my thirty-ninth birthday, without Kevin and Naomi being here.

"My #1 Is Still My #1!"

11 P.M.

I can breathe easier now as I prepare for our nightly fellowship. Thank You for directing me to make preparations for this trip last month, it really is on time and is very much needed. I have packed for my trip to Connecticut tomorrow and I am looking forward to our intimate time of fellowship together while away from Miriam and family obligations. I can think clearer without distractions and I can't wait to hear what You have planned for me as we move into 2003. Hallelujah! I made it through today! Thank you, Lord!!

JANUARY

1/1/2003

1:55 A.M.

I've just returned from Watch Night, New Year's Eve service, at Kainos with Miriam. She is fast asleep after I prayed over her. I'm fresh off of a *"praise high"* from testifying about how You, alone, are my Keeper. I gave You Praise, Honor, and Glory for Miriam's healing, my healing, my sanity, and my desire to spend New Years with You, yet again; after all we went through on last year.

I decided as I was driving home that if I am to move forward and stay with my face towards my destiny, I must forget about the circumstances of Kevin and Nne's death. I can't continue to rehearse the details of the accident because it only makes me anxious and is not productive. I must press forward, forgetting those things which are in my past, Kevin and Naomi's transition to life with You, and think on the plans You have for me and Miriam to prosper us in 2003!!

Lord, Lord, Lord! You have brought me out to a wealthy place and I have seen my promotion from lack to prosperity in the past eleven months. *You have truly blessed me!* 3 John 2 is alive in me as a testimony of my finances prospering as my soul and my health prospered. *You have proven Yourself faithful!* I have had some lessons to learn in 2002 and I pray that You were pleased by the decisions I made last year. Continue to guide me in the way I should go, allow me to recognize You and Your hand in the paths I must take, and not to be afraid to acknowledge You for what You have done in my life. Lord, give me wisdom in managing my time so that I can accomplish all that *You have predestined for me to do.* I can do it all through You, Christ, as You strengthen me!

Yesterday, I returned from my trip to Connecticut away from Houston, Miriam, and the church. It was totally refreshing! I had fun hanging out with my girlfriend, Evelyn (who I met at the old church), and acting like we were young, carefree girls again! I visited some major sites in New York City and You allowed me to purchase my *first* fur coat, MINK!!

As I gazed at myself in the mirror with the coat on, *I remembered all the years I went without a **new** coat when I was married* because I always deferred to Kevin and Naomi. Kevin was always going out for the Pastorate at a church and he needed to look dapper. Naomi was my growing child, so *she was going to get what she needed when she needed it.* I would make the sacrifice of buying myself a new coat so that we could buy for them. I used to wear the coats Kevin had out grown as my coat, even if it was too big for me. Now look at me! I can buy my own self a new coat and because of You, I got the desire of my heart – MINK! It is a full length, all female brown mink coat that looks great on me! It is a sure fire, head turning, show stopping, stunning garment that ***You bought for me!*** I pondered how I would share the great news about my mink coat with family and friends, and You gave me the words to say within twenty four hours!

You see me as an Ambassador of Christ and I have to represent Your Kingdom with the very best. My prosperity is a testimony of how You take care of Your own. I wanted to lie and say that my friend, Evelyn, had bought it for me. Then, I thought to say Kevin had bought it for me before he died. Then, ***You said*** that if I give the glory, honor and credit to someone else, then they would have to keep on blessing me ***and*** maintain my current blessings! Immediately, I repented and remembered that the blessings of God come with persecutions. (Mark 10:30) I need to study up on this Scripture in preparation for Your continual financial blessings because persecutions will come! *People will misjudge me and jump to conclusions.* Lord, You alone know that I can't defend my every purchase, nor do

I need to! Thank You, Jesus! Lord, toughen me up in this area so that *__I can stand to be blessed!__*

I told my sister Charlotta on last night (12/31/02) about the mink coat and I felt Your anointing on me real strong when I told her that **You allowed me to purchase it.** I knew right then and there that GOD and GOD alone, deserves all the credit for this gift - *not Kevin or anyone else!*

You are the One that exchanged beauty for my ashes! You are the Lifter of my head! Hallelujah! Hallelujah! Hallelujah! Thank You, Jesus! Hallelujah! I can't stop shouting!

Lord, it is 2:26A.M. on New Year's morning and I need to go to bed! Help me to calm down from all of this shouting. Hallelujah!

11 P.M.

Lord, my (DREAMS) goals for this year are:

1. To complete two books - ***"My #1 Is Still My #1!"*** and ***"... But God!"***
2. To prepare to leave my professional job so that I can devote myself full time to You for writing, teaching, and speaking engagements on behalf of Your ministry through me.
3. To continue my personal emotional healing and journey through grief.
4. To begin my doctorate study in Christian Education or Christian Counseling.
5. To become licensed in the ministry.
6. To manage my time better to minister to Miriam's needs and the assignment You have given me at Kainos Community Church.
7. To become more comfortable in being prosperous!

Lord these are all attainable goals through the Power of the Holy Ghost, Your Spirit, and not by my might!

"My #1 Is Still My #1!"

1/5/03

Lord, Jesus, Help Me!

When I think about Nne I get weak! I feel like I've been punched in the stomach and the wind has been knocked out of me. I cry out to You to SAVE ME from this despair, I long to think on only the positive memories. Teach me how to immediately exchange these negative emotions to overcome my grief over losing my firstborn, Naomi Eliza Dickey.

O Lord, My God, You know my grief because you lost your firstborn and only Son! *"Jesus, be a fence all around me everyday!"* (Same titled song by Fred Hammond) *I need You to protect me along life's way - keep me, guide me* - be my strong tower in the midst of this *first* anniversary of the accident season.

I want to remain in forward motion - maintaining my stride. Help me Lord to keep my face like flint towards the mark of the high calling in Christ Jesus. *Ooooh-wee! "Lord, I need Thee, every hour, I need Thee, oh bless me now, my Savior, I come to Thee!!"* (The chorus from the same titled song written by Annie S. Hawks that's in my heart)

10:43 P.M.

Thank You, Lord, for encouraging me through Your Word. **Your Word, _alone_, sustains me!!** I feed continuously on my IV medicine which is Your Word preached to my listening ears through T.D. Jakes, Joyce Meyer, Paula White, and Charles Stanley. I've feasted on Your Word this whole weekend and You have rewarded me for my time by strengthening me through Your Word!! I needed a booster shot in my soul and spirit to not give in to the depression and grief over the upcoming anniversary of the accident at the end of this month. Thank You for organizing my day and weekend!

"My #1 Is Still My #1!"

1/10/03

OK, Lord, I put in a request for time off from work. I want to use this time off for us to spend time together working towards my emotional healing. Today was officially my last day of work. I asked to be off on FMLA leave until March. I feel relieved that I am not under that obligation. I can drop Miriam off to school and return home to fellowship with You all day, work through my grief and depression, and finish the two books You began writing through me on last year.

I know I must rehearse the painful memories and walk through the doors I slammed shut in my heart because it hurt too badly last year. The only path to being totally healed is to walk through those doors. Lord, God, help me! Strengthen me! You alone, Jehovah, know what I'm about to go through and You alone can escort me. **I am scared to go through, to tell You the truth!** The thought of going through this makes my stomach ache, makes me anxious, and all around sick to my head and stomach to even think about the emotional work I have ahead of me.

Help me, Holy Ghost!! You, alone, are my Healer, empty me of my grief and sorrow so that You can fill me with Your love to overflowing! Lord, minister to me; relieve me of my headaches, stomachaches, and insomnia. I know I have been holding back because of my professional duties and parenting responsibilities and I need to let it out, let it go, and let You comfort me with your Holy Spirit. I am calling on all of heaven to please help me come through this grieving process!

1/11/03

A. M. Revelation

God used my old church to get "Egypt" (carnality) out of me, so that I would know how to treat other people. (People with spiritual authority over me, people in leadership, people as peers, people as new converts and members, *to not repeat* their evil behavior and gross mistreatment of others like they did to me and my family)

"My #1 Is Still My #1!"

P. M. Revelation

God began weaning me from depending on Kevin for my spiritual nourishment in '99. He moved me to begin depending on Him more than Kevin when He allowed me to shepherd the women's ministry at the church. Then in 2000 when I was at home on disability due to my difficult pregnancy with Miriam, God taught me how to diligently seek Him. He taught me how to allow Him to comfort me while I was home alone. He showed me that I could supplement my personal Bible study and church attendance with a more intimate and personal fellowship with Him on my own at home.

When we (me/Miriam) were left at home on Wednesdays and Sundays after she was born, I learned to fellowship with God and seek His strength to get me through that lonely season until I could rejoin the local fellowship. When I did rejoin the fellowship, I realized that I wasn't as satisfied with that experience as I was home alone with God. He allowed me *"to know"* that it was going to be me/Miriam and Kevin/Nne as teams in this family. I became grateful for the bond that developed between me and Mmi and accepted my assignment as Miriam's *chief guardian.* I was secure in the knowledge that Kevin had Nne, while I had Mmi and so it remains...

I am trusted by You for guardianship of Mmi. I have been proven trustworthy, thought highly of by You, and a benefactor of Your tremendous favor for this assignment. This is what I perceive in my spirit. Although, I don't see anything outwardly, I know You are supernaturally at work in my life. The more silent You are, the more You are at work behind the scenes. Help me to remain patient and strong as I continue to stand on Your promises made to me over the last few years. I need strength to "see with spiritual eyes" the end of this vision that ***shall*** ***come to pass***.

*"Surely I have calmed and quieted my soul, like a weaned child with my mother, like a weaned child **is** my soul within me." (Psalm 131:2, NKJV)* This is the verse I found to recite over and over to quiet my anxious soul as I take this grief journey with You.

1/12/03

Taking time off from work is my strategy to conquer the spiritual assassin of depression before the one year anniversary of the accident. My God, and my time spent with God, will lift me above and allow me to overcome this weapon of depression! I am a Warrior! I am a Conqueror! I have already defeated this enemy, now it is time to finish him off! For greater is He that is within me, than he that is in the world! (1 John 4:4) I'm confident with You on my side God, *that **I will** overcome this depression, Yes!*

P. M. Revelation

Lord, today You used the willing vessels at Kainos Community Church to love on me once again! The Pastors shared my ongoing struggle with depression during altar time. Then, Your vessels swooped down on me with loving kindness, to stand with me, and in prayer for me, to overcome and conquer this demon of depression! ***I am an overcomer!!***

1/13/03

Lord,
I am really trying to go to sleep, but can't! Every time I close my eyes my mind races. I feel like I am tuning in more to my emotions from 1/31/02 and I remember that I was asleep when the tragic accident was happening that day. It was a fitful and restless sleep for me, and my stomach ached throughout the sleep. That is how I feel right now; I'm having the same feeling that I had when I used to try to go to sleep after the accident. I couldn't sleep because when I woke up that first time after the accident, my entire world had changed! Thank God, I'm not shaking convulsively like I did back then, but there are still knots in my stomach that make me feel sick and ill.

Do I need to go see the wrecked car? I'm trying to decide do I need to? Guide me Lord!

By listing what I am grieving, I recognize that I not only lost my husband and daughter, I lost intimate relationships, dreams, and collective goals for our future, and our vision as a family. I have been shaken to my core, my center (Jesus) is holding me all together, but I feel like things all around me are falling apart, again.

The stress of trying to work, care for Miriam, write my books, lead a ministry at church, and going back to school as well as trying to take care of myself while grieving began to suffocate me. I felt like I was drowning and had to throw off everything just to come up for air. Now that I have laid down everything else, my head popped above water again. Just by staying home and not going to work today, relieved me from the stress of others' expectations.

If I wanted to cry, (which I did), and not put up a "game" face for observers, I could do so. I can think more clearly, now, and I can wait to hear from You. (You are silent again) I could be alone with my thoughts and recall my feelings, explore them, and wait for Your direction on them rather than running away with my own thoughts. I could regain control of my body by exercising, being disciplined in my eating, and feeding on Your Word. These disciplines add weight to my core center (Jesus) to keep me upright and afloat!!

P. M. Revelation

I was looking at Mmi's first birthday pictures and I remembered when I was taking those pictures at the restaurant and how Kevin didn't want to be in the pictures *__AT ALL!!__* He was almost hostile in his insistence that he *__NOT be photographed!__* In my spirit, I said to myself *"that's alright,"* because it was just me and Mmi in the picture. Even Nne had run away from the camera saying she didn't want to be in on Mmi's first birthday picture. I couldn't understand why they were tripping, but all the while, I kept saying to myself well, *"you and your Dad are a team and Mmi and I are a team."* These pictures will show who wanted to be together and who didn't. Again, I thought the reference was to us as teams in the family, not a prophecy over our lives.

Just like the time I got a knot in my stomach the day Kevin showed me this new route home from Light Christian Academy that brought us over the railroad tracks at Craven's Road. Coming up onto the tracks (where they were impacted), was when my own spirit cringed within me. My heart literally sank when I saw this new route and I asked him did it really cut down on the travel time home. We timed it and it did cut the time off by five minutes when compared to the Hwy 90 route. The same aching feeling that I felt while sleeping, during the exact time of the day they were in the accident, was the same awful cringe I felt within my spirit that day he showed me the new route and later on when the lawyers brought me back to the scene of the accident to show me what Kevin saw. As I reflect on it all now, I recognize three different instances of surrealism with the same dreadful forebodings. It was almost like God was trying to give me a warning in my subconscious spirit, but I still didn't "get it." **I NEVER** ever would have thought that my **"previewed vision"** over the railroad tracks would be how it would end for half of my family!!

In hindsight, I remember all the unctions from the Holy Spirit that I felt about that route, which was the reason I never took that new route. I've been remembering them for a while now. I just didn't have the courage to write the details of them down; as if that would have prevented the accident from occurring if I had shared them with Kevin...

I remember deciding to call Kevin to tell him I would pick up the girls from school that day, 1/31/02, but I heard a loud **"NO!"** come from the inside of my belly - like an inward rebuke of correction telling me not to cross in front of an oncoming car and I responded, "*OK, OK!*" The voice (Holy Spirit) said to go home and rest, pray, and wait for them. So I obeyed, never calling Kevin to chat like we usually did for his ride home. I prayed, read the Scriptures for that day for our church fast, and fell into a deep sleep at 5:25 P.M. I had a fitful sleep and woke up at 5:35 P.M. and 5:40 P.M. and finally just got up at 5:45 P.M. to get our meal on the table for us to end our church fast together as a family, at 6:00 P.M. their usual arrival time home like we normally did.

I sat down at the table after I got the plates set out and watched the six o'clock news. I realized they were late because they usually got home before the 6 P.M. news every night. As I watched the news, their lead in story was a tragic accident where a middle-aged man and his teenage daughter were killed when their vehicle was hit by a train. They said he was trying to beat the train, I couldn't believe it, *how could anyone think they could out run a train?* Nevertheless, I prayed for the family that was waiting for their loved ones (these two people) to come home, not knowing they had already died.

At this point, I decided to call Kevin to tell him ***not to take that new route*** because of the traffic build up due to the tragic auto-train accident. I felt like I had been restrained or held back from calling him earlier and my inner voice (Holy Spirit) finally released me to call him. I called him and he didn't answer. That seemed strange to me because he usually answered his cell phone on the first or second ring and now it just rang and rang. My heart started racing and the inner voice told me to eat now because I would need my strength later, so again, I obeyed while redialing Kevin's number and watching the news.

When I had finished eating, the news had an update that stated an infant baby girl was rescued from the wreck before the vehicle exploded and that she was in critical condition at an area Fort Bend Hospital. The car had exploded!! The victims were burned beyond any recognition!! My mouth dropped open as *I saw the back of <u>our</u> SUV* on the TV and it registered that **they were talking about MY FAMILY! I was numbed and paralyzed!**

I called Light Christian Academy (the girls' school) to find out what time they had left and Ms. Taylor, the director, told me they had left at 5:20 P.M. (giving them enough time to make it to the railroad tracks in time to get hit by 5:30 P.M!)

My world was <u>ROCKED</u>!

They were talking about Kevin and Naomi! He wasn't middle-aged and she was only ten years old!! Where did they get their information on the victims' ages from? How could Kevin try to beat a train? Did he really do what they said he did? How could he take that kind of chance with his life and our kids? No-no-no-no!

They had to have made a mistake! It only looks like my car with the same details about my family – a man and two girls - one infant and one of school age. Kevin was way too responsible to take that type of a risk, wasn't he? Lord, God, Lord, God, what is going on? I thought as long as they don't come to my house, it's not true, if the police don't come then it's not my family and he is stuck in traffic somewhere and can't hear his cell phone, that's it! That's the story I am sticking with, because the other one *can't be true!!*

But the police *did knock* on my door as I rationalized with myself about what had just happened. The policeman tries to tell me through the door about what happened, *but I tell him!* (I've begun shutting down emotionally and erecting protective walls to insulate me from this trauma.)

I think to myself, *"I - have - got - to - get - myself - together..."* (My thoughts begin trailing off).

I had spent myself emotionally on the floor shouting at God, fussing at Him for not protecting my family against this train wreck and asking, *"Why me?"* again? Why do I need this testimony twice? What are You trying to do in my life that necessitates this type of pain and trauma? What do I do now, God? What now?

The officer tells me I have to go to the hospital to see Mmi. I asked him to bring me. He refused and asked me who I knew who could drive me there. My mind went blank, my mind went all the way back to the accident with my parents sixteen years ago and I lost all sense of time. In my mind, I was alone, single, just arrived in Houston after graduating college and didn't know ANYBODY!

My mind snapped back to the present when my neighbors came over to help me. All I could do was ask them to pray with me, pray for me, and pray that Miriam would make it through her injuries with minimum scarring. I had no idea that **that prayerful moment** cancelled the assignment the enemy had on her. I arrived at the hospital to find her just like we prayed for with minimum injuries and scarring, Hallelujah!!

Kevin and Naomi were together in heaven and Miriam and I were together on earth and so it is to this day!

1/14/03

Lord,

I realized today that I never got a chance to say good-bye to any of my loved ones before they died! They were all snatched away

"My #1 Is Still My #1!"

from me without my ever being present at any of their transitions. Dad's accident, Mom's aneurysm, Kevin and Naomi's accident all happened with me not being there to witness their departure.

I was allowed to see one of the church members, Sister Hodge's, transition while at our first ever Women's Retreat for the old church in Galveston, TX and I handled that one pretty well. Lord, I thought You could trust me to be present at the transition of Christian loved ones after that experience.

Then, 1/31/02 arrived and I was at home trying to sleep, while my own family was transitioning from life to death to life with You. What happened that I was left outside of the loop, again? Granted, that accident scene was horrific and could have taken me out mentally if I had survived and witnessed it, but You, alone, know what You are doing, God, You alone know!

I am exhausted from my tears. My head, neck, and body are tense and the tears offer me some physical relief even though I feel I am still holding back. I haven't released them fully yet but they are on their way. I want to undergo this grief recovery process, get over it and come through this! I don't want to stuff my feelings down anymore and not deal with them; I want to work through this, Lord, please Help Me!

1/15/03

A. M. Revelation
Lord,

I'm not fearful of this trial I'm going through, just weary! Strengthen me, Lord! I'm feeding my spirit man, inflate me, and lift me above my circumstances so that I can soar!! God *is* working everything out in my life! Even when all is quiet! Look at how You have encouraged me with these Scriptures to hang in there. Your comfort to me, while I wait on You, You are moving, even when it doesn't look like it.

*"My #1 **Is Still My #1!**"*

Luke 4:18-19, (NCV)

The Lord has put his Spirit in me,
> *because he appointed me to tell the Good News to the poor.*

He has sent me to tell the captives they are free
> *and to tell the blind that they can see again.*

God sent me to free those who have been treated unfairly
> *and to announce the time when the Lord will show his kindness.*

Isaiah 60:14-15, (NCV)

The people who have hurt you will bow down to you;
> *those who hated you will bow down at your feet.*

They will call you The City of the LORD,
> *Jerusalem, and city of the Holy One of Israel.*

You have been hated and left empty
> *with no one passing through.*

But I will make you great from now on;
> *you will be a place of happiness forever and ever.*

Isaiah 60:18-20, (NCV)

There will be no more violence in your country;
> *it will not be ruined or destroyed.*

You will name your walls Salvation
> *and your gates Praise.*

The sun will no longer be your light during the day
> *nor will the brightness from the moon be your light,*

Because the LORD will be your light forever,
> *and your God will be your glory.*

Your sun will never set again,
> *and your moon will never be dark,*

Because the LORD will be your light forever,
> *and your time of sadness will end.*

Hallelujah! These are my promises!

All of a sudden my breakout will come forth speedily, with a twofold recompense. Hallelujah!

Isaiah 61: 1-3; 7-8, (NCV)

*The Lord G*OD *has put his Spirit in me,*
    *because the L*ORD *has appointed me to tell the good news to the poor.*
He has sent me to comfort those whose hearts are broken,
    to tell the captives they are free,
    and to tell the prisoners they are released.
*He has sent me to announce the time when the L*ORD *will show his kindness*
    and the time when our God will punish evil people.
He has sent me to comfort all those who are sad
    and to help the sorrowing people of Jerusalem.
I will give them a crown to replace their ashes,
    and the oil of gladness to replace their sorrow,
    and clothes of praise to replace their spirit of sadness.
Then they will be called Trees of Goodness,
    *trees planted by the L*ORD *to show his greatness.*
Instead of being ashamed, my people will receive twice as much wealth.
    Instead of being disgraced, they will be happy because of what they receive.
They will receive a double share of the land,
    so their happiness will continue forever.
*I, the L*ORD, *love justice.*
    I hate stealing and everything that is wrong.
I will be fair and give my people what they should have,
    and I will make an agreement with them that will continue forever.

The promise from God of Supernatural Refreshing in His Presence! Hallelujah!!

Isaiah 40:28-31, (NCV)

Surely you know.
     Surely you have heard.
The LORD is the God who lives forever,
     who created all the world.
He does not become tired or need to rest.
     No one can understand how great his wisdom is.
He gives strength to those who are tired
     and more power to those who are weak.
Even children become tired and need to rest,
     and young people trip and fall.
But the people who trust the LORD will become strong again.
     They will rise up as an eagle in the sky;
     they will run and not need rest;
     they will walk and not become tired.

Psalm 23:1-3, (NCV)

The LORD is my shepherd;
     I have everything I need.
He lets me rest in green pastures.
     He leads me to calm water.
He gives me new strength.
     He leads me on paths that are right
     for the good of his name.

Psalm 119:37, (NCV)

Keep me from looking at worthless things.
     Let me live by your word.

Acts 3: 19, (NCV)

So you must change your hearts and lives! Come back to God, and he will forgive your sins. Then the Lord will send the time of rest.

P. M. Revelation

Lord,

I just planted a large seed offering to Daystar Television Network to have my lawsuit against the railroad settled in my favor. The guest minister, Mike Murdock, prophesied to a young single mother **(ME)** who was having a hard time raising her child alone and has a lawsuit pending*!* He prophesied that if she (I) sowed an offering it would be settled in my favor!! I had already planted the seed and was thinking of what harvest I expected from it and after I thought in my head *"The lawsuit settled in my favor,"* Mike Murdock spoke it! His prophecy dropped in my spirit like an anchor and it hit the bottom of my soul - I couldn't stop shouting! I shouted for about five minutes!

<u>My Lord</u>*!!* I hollered and screamed <u>*so LOUD*</u>! My heart was racing a mile a minute like I had literally *been running for Jesus!* I was so excited for the confirmation! I sat down to write out my budget for giving this year. I want to scatter seed as a sower and decided which additional ministries I will give regularly to this year. I figured out that my giving budget (offerings) will match or supersede my tithes this year, not counting almsgiving.

I have always wanted my offerings to match my tithes or supersede them and this year I will be able to do it!! *How ironic I am able to do it because of the accident,* **now *I can afford to do it!*** I know that You give seed to the sower. I just want **more seed** <u>to sow more seeds</u>, *for* <u>*I am*</u> *a seed sower!*

1/16/03

Lord,

I have realized from listening to You in our quiet time that I wasn't living a balanced life. I was busy, busy, busy, taking care of Miriam, working, and teaching in the ministry at church, and didn't schedule any time for myself or regular R&R. The stretches between my devotions were too long and contributed to my weariness. This left me off balanced, off kilter, and lopsided. I longed to spend quality time with You on a regular basis, but I felt hurried and rushed during our times together. My days were running into one another and I constantly felt behind, sometimes two to three days behind. I needed time to myself, not to feel so rushed everyday. I needed to plan my days and organize my time better, right?

I do know I feel refreshed and refocused just by spending more time in Your presence. It really is making a difference in my mental and emotional state. *Thank You!* A quote that came to me by email was *"Sorrow looks back, worry looks around, but faith looks up."*

I feel a relief in the spiritual atmosphere, the cloud of depression that oppressed me on last week has dissipated and I feel relieved. I don't know if it was because I'm taking leave from my job, intercessory prayer, or everything working together for my good, like in Romans 8:28, but I definitely do feel relieved of my stressors this week. Thank You, God!!

Guess what I'm using to keep me warm tonight? My new mink coat! I walked through the house talking to Kevin and Naomi showing it off to them. The temperature has dropped in Houston and when Kevin was alive he declared it, *"breaking in new wives"* weather, and time to cuddle and make love to keep warm. Remembering that little tidbit reminded me of why I miss him immensely. Because of Your love of me through him, I experienced what true love feels like and I know what I'm missing and would trade this mink coat for him in a heartbeat.

When I look back at our wedding pictures, I can't believe he's not here with me anymore. No more! **No** more! **No More**! I only have this coat to keep me WARM in this midnight hour. It looks good, feels good, and is good! I feel like *I should have been had* this mink coat a long time ago, like when Kevin was alive to enjoy it with me. Now he's gone and I have to settle for this mink coat, ***all alone***, oh well!

1/17/03

Lord,

Today I learned the name of my emotional state; I learned that I have been battling anxiety, depression, and grief due to post traumatic stress disorder (PSTD). Daily, I plead the Name of Jesus and the power in the blood of Jesus against this three fold cord. I pray that by the grace of God, as well as the intercessory prayers I am receiving through all of the prayer warriors, that this spirit be cursed to its root! For no weapon formed against me shall prosper, it won't work! (Isaiah 54:17, NKJV) ***God You have been so-o faithful!*** I didn't know how much relief I would feel just by giving up work during this stressful season. My mind is so much clearer and I can now focus better on the other details I have to attend to. You really did order this rest for me and I am relieved, thank You!

1/18/03

Lord,

We (Mmi and I) are awake already and it's 5:30 A.M. in the morning! She's ready to start her day now and asked me to let her brush her teeth, fix her cereal for breakfast and I don't know what next, but ***I would like to go BACK to sleep***! Lord, here is my body *please* use it to minister to Mmi. I want to lie down, but You have to raise it up to be used in service to Mmi right now. **Help!**

1/20/03

Lord,

You allowed me the grace/power to minister to Mmi this entire weekend, thank You, Jesus!! And again, today when she woke up early between 6:30 - 7:00 A.M. Hallelujah for Your strength, Lord!

"My #1 Is Still My #1!"

On my way to Mia's church tonight, I felt a tugging on my heart, like a wooing from You, as I made my way to service. They had prepared a foot washing ceremony for us to participate in and it reminded me of what had happened to me the last two times I washed somebody's feet and how they died afterwards. After I washed Sister Hodges' feet during the old church's first women's retreat in Galveston, she died a few hours later. The night before Kevin's accident, I ministered to him by rubbing and massaging his feet and he died the next day. My head and my heart couldn't remember the incredible honor I felt as I ministered to both Kevin and Sister Hodges in this servant manner. I was just paralyzed with fear by the thought of washing someone else's feet and the possibility of them dying afterwards. I became emotionally numbed, but I still went through the motions of foot washing anyway.

As I ministered, I was praying that the sister whose feet I washed would have a tender heart towards God again, but it really was a prayer for me. The offenses and the hurts that I've endured from last year have caused my heart to harden. I need to exchange this stony heart for one of flesh. I want to be tender hearted for You, Lord, and not to be so hard hearted and calloused by the moves of God, again. I know that I felt an anointing on the way there tonight. I know that I felt the tugging of the Holy Ghost on my heart.

Even before we began, I was reminded of some anger, resentment, and bitterness that I'm still working on from my time at the old church as well as residual anger towards Kevin. I don't know why the devil brought that up right before the service. I thought that me and You had settled that last year and here he goes bringing up old stuff. Yes, I was angry at Kevin for choosing the church over me and for running himself ragged showing love towards people who were too selfish to respect him or his family. Kevin allowed them to mistreat us, and I lost respect for him for not standing up to them in defense of our family or himself. But, I still acknowledge that I didn't know then, and nor do I know now, Your plan and workings in that situation. Kevin maintained that You called him to that church and I supported him in his decision even though I personally did not care for the way things happened to him or the family. We were totally disregarded by the leadership team and You reminded

"My #1 Is Still My #1!"

me that their mistreatment of me after the accident was an extension of their disrespect for our family. It's 2003 and I want to move on past last year and quit dwelling on the past. Help me, God, to remain focused on today and *this* year!

I want the restoration with the increase You have promised me in 2003. **<u>ABSOLUTELY EVERYTHING</u>**, *You have stored up for me in 2003!!* I want the luxury car, the favorable settlement of the lawsuit and as nourishment for my soul and for this **whole** experience I want *Psalm 131:2* to become real in my life.

Psalm 131:2 says, "But I have learned to feel safe and satisfied just like a young child on its mother's lap." (My own translation)

1/22/03

Lord,

Like Jacob said in Genesis 32:26, I'm not going to let You go until You bless me! **I won't settle for anything less than total restoration with future increase of no less than DOUBLE for my trouble**! I am contending with God, (vs.28), and have power with God and men and have prevailed. I, like Jacob, come boldly, incessantly, to You! God, I come like the widow woman who continued to petition the judge to avenge her of her adversary in Luke 18:3. Just like the judge gave in to her persistence, You, God promise to defend, protect, and avenge me speedily, if I persist. (Luke 18:8) I haven't fainted, lost heart, or given up on my expectation that You will redeem me, Your chosen, elect one, who cries out to You day and night! I'm still waiting for Romans 8:28! I have prayed for Your mercy, Your grace, Your strength to endure, and wisdom to make it out through this test and trial of my faith. (1 Corinthians 10:13)

Lord, I won't ever stop asking You to help me! I am standing in faith, even for crumbs, just like the Canaanite woman in Matthew 15:27. I want to impress upon You my faith to believe that You, alone, can heal me! You, alone, can deliver me! You, alone, can restore me! You, alone, can equip me, and send me forth, after You have healed me, to heal others! (2 Corinthians 1:4) I receive Luke 11:9 as instructions on how to boldly, shamelessly, persistently, and insistently pray to You.

Help me to walk in love according to Galatians 5:6. Lord, I am putting pressure on Your Word like in Matthew 7:12 because that's what I want! *I have given first* and expect it to come back to me! I gave seed of a car in '95 to Jeanette and Earl as a second car for them because they had a baby (Earl III) on the way. I call **that faith seed** to come forth as a LUXURY CAR for me! I've committed seed offerings above my tithes, which are more than I give in tithes, so that Your law of seed time and harvest would manifest in my life in 2003! **I want to receive *my* inheritance, *Kevin's* inheritance, and *Naomi's* inheritance to spend wisely for Your Kingdom**. I will be a wise steward of Your possessions and I pray that how I have invested your seed last year proves to You that *I can be trusted with more!*

11:30 P.M.

Lord,

All of the things I am anticipating this year in You have me real excited! I can't wait to walk in them! I only ache and grieve for Kevin because he's not here to share in this with me. I am experiencing one of the highest moments of my life spiritually and he's not here to share it with me. We prayed and believed You for many years to bring us into our destiny and promise, not knowing we wouldn't share it together. I shared in his, but he's not here to share in mine. I am left to grieve the loss, the companionship, and fellowship of not having him present to share my momentous occasions. He's missing them, I'm getting ready to walk into the promises You prepared for me since before the foundation of time and my partner of the past twelve and a half years won't be here to share in this harvest.

But to be truthful, in all of the visions You showed me of me ministering, *I NEVER SAW* Kevin in them! I asked You, how it could be that such great opportunities for me would go unaccompanied by my significant other and I never got an answer. It didn't seem right that my husband would be absent from **every vision** You allowed me to preview. He should have been there for me, present to support me and it made *no sense* in my visions for him not to be there! Now, I understand more clearly what was cloudy in the vision. He wasn't present because he was *no longer present! He was deceased!* And I was being used in ministry without him! Hmph, hmph, hmph! *(Another punch to my gut.)*

We weren't ministering together or separately! Our season as a team was over and I was doing it solo with one daughter. I never thought about it again when I became pregnant with Mmi, *who looks just like Naomi.* I forgot about the visions and plans You had for me, not to harm me but to prosper me as in Jeremiah 29:11. Now, here I am in 2003, ministering solo with one daughter, Miriam, without my husband, Kevin, just like I saw in my vision! **It has come to pass!**

1/24/03

Yes!! I got a revelation from You today, as I was exercising on the treadmill, on how to break the back of unforgiveness off of me! I am ***to literally bless*** my enemies, the old church and leaders! I have resisted that suggestion from You for four months because I did not want to condone their mistreatment of me and my family. But today, I realized that the cost of my freedom, from this tormenting demon of unforgiveness, is to make an offering to the old church that despised me and my family to cancel out their debt owed to me! I have no expectations attached to this gift, a commercial refrigerator, that I know is really needed by the church. I know this is the thing to do! As soon as I decided to obey, I felt lighter like the spiritual weight and chains of unforgiveness finally fell off of me, Hallelujah, I'm free!!!

1/27/03

Lord,

As I attempted to follow through on the love offering of the commercial refrigerator to my former church, I ran into resistance from the leaders. None of them would return my calls to find out what I wanted. I am so determined to give them this gift so that I could be free from unforgiveness, that I spoke with the church musician (the same lady who accompanied me to the hospital to get Miriam last year) and asked her to get information about the store they were trying to buy the refrigerator from, for me, so that I could pay for it. I can write the check to the church to reimburse them if they have already paid for it or I could write it out to the business! It doesn't matter to me! I am so FREE from this demon of unforgiviness that their usual rude behavior towards me didn't even bother, nor discourage me from pressing on to bless them! Hallelujah! Thank You, Lord! I've been shouting all weekend over this deliverance! Yes, Lord, I'm free!!!

Today, I also began teaching my Sunday morning class titled, *"The Bait of Satan,"* a curriculum I developed from the book by John Bevere dealing with offenses. I was delivered from offenses after reading that book and was so glad about it that I wanted to teach others how to do it! I'm finally free from the spirits of grief, anger, fear, depression, resentment, bitterness, and now unforgiveness that descended on me when tragedy entered my life on 1/31/02.

Your love poured out of me as I ministered to the class on *"The Bait of Satan."* Your anointing reduced all of us to liquid LOVE as the class members' hearts began to melt too! Thank You, Lord for giving me a tender heart after being brokenhearted! It is marvelous in my eyes to behold my own transformation! I can't believe it's me! I know it's Your love demonstrated through me! WOW! I now realize that everything You ask of me, **You strengthen me to do!** Hallelujah! God has restored me! He has ushered me into my emotional healing and victory in 2003! Hallelujah!!

You have continued to purge me of offenses, hurts and pain that I suffered on last year and I feel Your love – Your overwhelming love for me! I was finally freed to shout with my whole heart, all out, no holds, barred at my new church today! I shouted and screamed so much I passed out cold at the altar! That was alright! You were doing a healing work in me, again, and afterwards I got up restored from that altar! Hallelujah!

I never thought I could bless my old church with *anything* after the way we were treated while Kevin was alive. And after he died, when I thought I that I couldn't bear anymore pain – they gave me more! I was so angry and disappointed with them. And I was angry at YOU for allowing me to endure such mistreatment from them after Kevin and Naomi's home going.

But, through my own persistent time in prayer, waiting on You, and intercessory prayer from others, YOU have brought me around to sincerely wanting to bless my former church without malice, resentment, or bitterness, Hallelujah! Thank You, Jesus! I thank You that I am free from them! I know You freed me from my grief and sorrow over losing Kevin and Naomi in July 2002, at the *"Woman Thou Art Loosed"* Conference in Dallas, Texas.

This unforgiviness was a remnant left over from that loss. Last year I lost three things:

1. Kevin
2. Naomi
3. My church home

Now, I am delivered from my pain, hurt, and anger over all three of these losses. I can go on in 2003 without continuing to look back at 2002 and feeling the deep pain, hurt, and bruising that occurred because of the severe emotional and psychic trauma I experienced.

I still have emotional scars but they are healing. They remind me of my *"crucifixion with Christ"* and I look at last year and shake my head in awe that I am even ***still here,*** after all I came through to get here!! Miriam is physically healed with minimal scarring and her hair has grown back thicker than ever. Hallelujah! My prophecy over our lives has come to pass!

Last Sunday was one year to the day, not date that I last heard and saw Kevin preach at our former church. Last week was like my Holy Week, and this past Sunday was my own resurrection from the ashes of last year, it was my Easter Sunday!

God, my experience is parallel to Job (*I'm Jobeth*), Joseph (*I'm Josephina*), and Jesus Christ (*I'm a Christian*)! Job had to bless his miserable comforters in Chapter 42 before he received double for his trouble! Joseph realized that what the devil meant for evil, God meant for his (my) own good in Genesis 50. And Jesus was anointed ***"to come through"*** testing in the wilderness after His baptism and was ministered to by angels afterwards in Matthew 4, just like I have been! I, like Jesus, am anointed ***to come through my testing*****!!**

I am anointed to come through! Hallelujah!

I am still anointed to run on, to see what my end will be with my tender heart restored!! Hallelujah!! A heart tender towards You, God! You knew I would come through this, even when I doubted that I could! Even when I wanted to give up and clock out of this evil world, You kept me in my right mind, Lord!! Hallelujah!!

Thank You!! Thank You!! Thank You!! Thank You!! Thank You!! Thank You!!

I'm still here to testify of Your faithfulness! Your goodness! Self control! Love! Peace! Joy! Patience! Kindness! And gentleness! I have suffered in my flesh to birth this fruit, of Your Spirit! Lord, *have I ever suffered* and died to my flesh!!! ***I have come through*** this testing, steadfast in my faith, with a more thorough understanding of this Scripture from *James 1:2-4, (MSG).*

"Consider it a sheer gift, friends, when tests and challenges come at you from all sides. You know that under pressure, your faith-life is forced into the open and shows its true colors. So don't try to get out of anything prematurely. Let it do its work so you become mature and well-developed, not deficient in any way."

I mentally rehearsed in my mind that this was to produce mature endurance and a deeper sense of dependence on God to whom I turned to for wisdom and strength to endure!

My journey began, alone with God in this house, as I found out about the accident on TV from the six o'clock news. God and I, together, are culminating the end of a year of *"firsts..."* one on one in this house. This Friday will be the *first* year anniversary date, 1/31/03, of Kevin and Naomi's transition to heaven. I'm finally submitting to doing the emotional work needed to complete my journey through grief!

Thank You, Lord, for being patient with me!!!

1/31/03

O, My God, I finally got it!!! You trust me!
O, my God, <u>YOU</u> - <u>TRUST</u> - <u>ME</u>!

You've restored unto me, my desire to WORSHIP YOU!!! You trusted that I would go through this past year and *still worship YOU* despite everything!! In spite of all the evil spirits that tried to rule over me, **The Holy Spirit** *allowed me to emerge* **victorious as a Conqueror!!**
These tests and trials proved to me what was deposited in me!! That I had it in me to finish this course, Hallelujah!! **You trusted me to still desire to worship You, not just praise You,** *but worship You after all I've been through!! Hallelujah!!*

O God,
O God,
O God,
I can't believe You trusted me!!
I knew I could trust You, but I didn't know that <u>You</u> <u>could</u> <u>trust</u> <u>me</u>!!!

I came through this test of my faith still desiring to be with You, still worshipping You, still trusting You for my restoration, restitution, and recompense! And now I expect my reward for diligently seeking You, in my case, double for my trouble! At the very least quadruple (two deaths x double for my trouble) restoration, when You turn my captivity like you did for Job in Chapter 42:10.

I lost two loved ones and one church fellowship. Job lost his fortunes, family, and health and You gave him double for his trouble, Hallelujah!! I lift my hands, as well as my heart, to receive **ALL THAT YOU HAVE PROMISED ME, TODAY!!!** My spirit responds to the deep call of Your Spirit, and lines up in place to receive Your blessing for me **IN THIS SEASON!**

Even before the accident, I was a generous giver to God's Kingdom! Prosperity became a magnifier of my heart. The vow I made to You, I kept! I became an even bigger giver to Your Kingdom!

I proved that You could trust me to be a Distribution Center for Wealth.

What I have is seed because it is not enough for the end time harvest! To finance that harvest, I will need more money! You already know that!! So I sowed back into Your Kingdom and now my reaping has begun after a year of consistent sowing.

The spiritual breakthroughs that I am experiencing now are a direct result of my sowing financial seeds to meet my emotional needs for breakthroughs! Thank You for being Faithful! You are absolutely Awesome! My Deliverer! My Redeemer! My Vindicator! My Lord and my Savior!

I am free to worship You from deep down in my belly. I can feel the deep wellsprings overflow from the inside, pouring out of me. I have my tender heart back after all I've been through this past year! ***I have my tender heart back, YES!***

My spirit is singing the refrain from the song, *"Where He Leads Me,"* by E.W. Blandy:

Where He leads me, I will follow,
Where He leads me, I will follow,
Where He leads me, I will follow,
I'll go with Him, with Him, ALL THE WAY!!

"Without faith no one can please God. Anyone who comes to God must believe that he is real and that he rewards those who truly want to find him."(Hebrews 11:6, NCV)

My negative experiences didn't hide the Lord – they revealed Him because I desired to remain in right standing with God. I was in a place where the fire consumed everything except **my desire to know HIM**!

I gave up all the inferior stuff, so that I could know Christ personally! To be a partner in His sufferings, to experience His resurrection power, and to go all the way with Him!!!

My final reflection on this experience so far:

Worship is private and I <u>still</u> worship You, Lord! I praise You and thank You for trusting me – DUST – with this testimony! How awesome of You to trust Your treasured anointing in this earthen vessel named, Bernice Marie Bright Dickey!!! WOW!!!

"For our light affliction, which is but for a moment, is working for us a far more exceeding and eternal weight of glory,"
(2 Corinthians 4:17, NKJV)